Bringing Out the Potential of Children
Volume 2
Gardeners

Patrice Porter

Bringing Out the Potential of Children Gardeners

© Copyright 2017 Patrice Porter All rights reserved.

No part of this book may be reproduced or transmitted in any form or by any means, including but not limited to information storage and retrieval systems, electronic, mechanical, photocopy, recording, etc. without written permission from the copyright holder.

ISBN 978-1-7751178-2-7

Cover Design: Patrice Porter

DEDICATION

To my daughter-in-law and granddaughter, Jackie and Ffion. With much gratitude to Jackie, who has developed a wonderful, productive garden and opened the delights of gardening to Ffion at a very early age.

Table of Contents

Introduction

Chapter 1 Choosing Your Spot and Ensuring Those Beginning Successes..................................pg. 1

Chapter 2 Soil – Building a Good Foundation........ pg.17

Chapter 3 The Miracle of Seeds and the Emerging Seedlings..pg. 24

Chapter 4 Feeding and Watering Your Plants......... pg. 49

Chapter 5 Getting Rid of the Competition - Weeding and Thinning......................................pg. 54

Chapter 6 Doing Pest Control and Keeping Your Plants Disease Free...pg. 55

Chapter 7 Bringing In the Harvest and Preserving It...pg.18

Chapter 8 Reviewing Your Successes and Planning for Next Season.............................. pg. 91

About the Author..pg. 92

Appendix 1: "From the Ground Up"..............pg.93

Appendix 2: Garden Recipes......................... pg.104

INTRODUCTION

If you truly believe that our children are very capable learners and recognize the potential in them then this book is for you, to bring out the potential as gardeners, food producers.

I've always had a garden of some sort and loves fresh garden food. Being able to create an abundance of fresh produce in a garden is something I would want everyone to experience. Thus we have this book.

Bringing Out the Potential of Children. Gardeners.

- Discover the delight in sharing the miracle of growing - taking a tiny seed and nurturing it into a mature food producing plant with the sense of wonderment it brings out in the children.
- Start gardening and open the door to having access to good nutritious food and the feeling of satisfaction in producing that food.

This book will give all you need to get started in the growing process and sharing in the delight of being a food producer.

It covers all the way from choosing a gardening spot to bringing in the harvest. All done in a fun and inspiring way.

Chapter 1: Choosing Your Spot and Ensuring Those Beginning Successes

Give someone some fresh produce and they will eat for a day.
Teach them to garden and they will never be hungry.
They can have food to eat for a lifetime.
– modified from an old Chinese proverb

To start off you're going to need a special spot for your child to start growing in. This chapter deals with finding a good gardening spot and also what it takes for successful gardening. For it is with these beginning successes that lifelong gardeners are created.

To set your children up for success
- Start with a small plot that's easy for them to manage. Make it a spot of their very own even if that spot is just one container they are growing in. You can always add more containers later or expand their growing area when they are ready for it.
- Make sure they are involved in every aspect of the creation of their garden. By everything, I mean EVERYTHING - from the choosing of their gardening spot, planting and caring for their garden and be sure it's them who do the harvesting and bringing in their goodies to add to the table. No matter how small the contribution, it's important they see that they can add to the family food supply and well-being.

Setting your child up for success (cont.)

- Come prepared to help out a little 'behind the scene' with things they may not be ready for yet. You may need to do some pest control, or move the sprinkler around or perhaps some of the initial breaking of the ground. Let them do whatever they are capable of, remembering that the child's 'ownership' of the plot is the main thing.
- Never rush things. Give your child lots of time to explore, bringing out their sense of wonderment and curiosity. There is a whole lot happening in the garden they'll want to check out and you'll find there is no greater joy than that from a child who has cultivated plants in his or her own vegetable garden.
- A picture is worth a thousand words. Never tell kids something you could show them.

When choosing your garden spot

- Make it easily accessible for children but also where they can be viewed by others.
- Make sure it gets at least 6 hours of sunlight.
- Find a spot that is somewhat sheltered and out of the wind.

A fun project to do while you are tracking the sun, to let you know how much sun a certain spot will get, is to make up a sundial.

Here's two simple methods for making a **Sundial.**

Materials

- stick

- rocks or chalk

- 1 cup of playdough (optional)

- watch or clock

Find your sunny spot.

Put the stick in the ground. If it is a sidewalk or patio, put the stick in the playdough and use that to hold the stick upright on cement.

Throughout the day, place a rock, or mark with chalk for each hour indicating where the shadow falls at that time.

Now your sundial is ready to use. When you want to tell the time, just look for the shadow.

Simple Sundial.

Materials

- paper plate
- marker
- pencil
- watch or clock

Directions

Look at the numbers on a clock

Write those numbers down, evenly spaced around the paper plate for each hour.

Punch your pencil through the middle of the plate

Point the 12 due north and the sun should tell you what time it is or check the time and place the plate facing the directions that is showing that time.

What if you have no growing areas with full sun?
Try these shade tolerant plants.

Great shade-tolerant vegetables include:

Beets.

Carrots.

Chard.

Cilantro.

Garlic.

Kale.

Lettuce.

Bok Choy

Types of Herbs That Will Grow in the Shade

If you want to grow herbs indoors or in your backyard on the patio, you might struggle with having enough direct sunlight. Luckily, there are some herbs that grow excellent in the shade. Here are some herbs to add to your garden even when it has shade.

Parsley

Not a lot of herbs can grow well in the shade, but there are some really great ones that do! To start with, there is parsley, which is not only used in different medicinal recipes, but of course used in your favorite meals. It is great to have parsley on hand at all times, so you can keep it fresh in your kitchen, or even dry it to preserve it longer. You can even use the root of the parsley plant in soups and stews. Plus, it freshens your breath just by chewing on a parsley leaf.

Types of Herbs That Will Grow in the Shade (continued)

Mint

Who doesn't love mint? This is another excellent herb for growing in the shade, and works perfectly for indoor container gardening. Mint has a strong scent so it works as a natural deodorizer in the home, plus can be used for your own toothpaste, adding to recipes, or making some soothing tea. You want to make sure you keep your mint trimmed as it can get pretty big when it isn't pruned on a regular basis.

Chives

Chives are an excellent herb when you want to cook with more of your own fresh herbs, and can also grow in the shade. The leaves of the chive plant are used for various dishes, from your favorite soup, to topping salads. While chives do best in full sun, you can still grow them indoors in the shade or on the patio, as long as it is warm enough.

Types of Herbs That Will Grow in the Shade (continued)

Thyme

This is one of the more popular herbs to grow in general, so it is good news that you can even grow it in the shade. However, there are different types of thyme, and they don't all grow as well without direct sunlight. English thyme is usually the best option when you don't have a lot of direct sunlight for your herbs. You are able to use the entire herb for your cooking, but the leaves can also be used alone and you may throw away the stems, which are quite woody.

Tarragon

Another good herb for growing for your cooked dishes is tarragon. This can be grown in the shade, though at least a little sunlight is usually good if you can pull it off. This is a highly flowering plant so it also looks beautiful in your garden.

A good beginner's garden is a **container garden,** which can be more flexible and more mobile. This ability to move things let's you change them around with the changing seasons. Also container gardening can be done indoors in a sunny spot.

Nearly anything that holds soil and has good drainage can be used in **container gardening**. Let your child pick out some interesting pots and encourage him or her to decorate them. They can be anything from recycled yogurt container, old buckets to old school shoes, boot or sneakers!

How about growing your own salad bowl!

No, I'm not talking about the glass or wooden bowl sitting in your kitchen cabinet that you serve lettuce in. I'm talking about bowls or pots that you can grow your own lettuce and salad makings in.

You can repurpose an old traditional salad bowl to grow your lettuce in. Glass bowls don't work as well since it's impossible to add drainage holes in the bottom. Your wooden bowls should work well if you drill a hole in the bottom for drainage or use the pots you're no longer using for potted plants.

Growing your own salad bowl (cont.)

The basic idea is simple. You get a bowl or pot, fill it with potting soil, and plant your salad and salad fixings. A salad or lettuce bowl can include several different varieties of lettuce and a few of your favorite herbs. Or you can divide everything up in several different containers and grow a small tomato plant and a few green onions as well. Mix and match as you see fit, depending on what you like to eat.

That's the fun of growing your own food. You can try different varieties and combinations until you come up with the one that works best for you. Along the way, you get to sample and try different varieties of lettuce your local market doesn't offer. There's so much more than iceberg lettuce and spinach out there.

Salad bowls are small and compact way to give gardening a try. They are also an excellent tool to help teach your children about where our food comes from and how it is grown. Get the little ones involved in planting and caring for the lettuce plants. Not only is it a great learning experience, it's also a wonderful way to get them to eat more greens. After all, they've grown this lettuce.

These work great for growing indoors.

Growing your own salad bowl (cont.)

Lettuce plants don't have very deep roots, which is why shallow bowls work perfectly for planting them indoors. And since it won't get super-hot - even in a sunny window- you don't need a large amount of soil to retain moisture. In other words, shallow bowls are a great way to grow a large amount of lettuce in little space or soil.

To get started, get a nice shallow planting bowl and a bag of quality potting soil that includes a slow release fertilizer appropriate for vegetables. Or if you're composting already, well-aged compost would make a rich organic way to fertilize your lettuce. Get them started, watch them grow and harvest once they grow to maturity. Last but not least, eat and enjoy!

Consider also creating a special spot for storing your child's garden tools. It's wonderful for them to have their own child-sized shovels, rakes, hoes and some garden gloves or maybe their tools may be large spoons for digging and old measuring cups, bowls and pails for harvesting. A watering can of their own is great too.

Here's a simple **DIY watering can** made out of an old plastic bottle (1 gallon milk bottles are great because of the handle)

DIY Watering Can

Instructions:

Clean out a one gallon milk jug.

Heat a needle over match or lighter for a few seconds. Poke holes into the lid, reheat and repeat.

You can make one with a super fine/gentle spray by using a small needle and one with a more flow by using a bigger needle.

Fill with water and replace lid – Viola! A homemade watering can.

Now, getting down to the actual gardening part.

Tips:

- It's a good idea to spend only about 15 minutes per activity before changing tasks. Most kids love to water and plant things but usually not so much the weeding, mulching and thinning. Here's where this guideline comes in handy allowing you to say "Let's do 10 minutes of weeding, then you can grab your watering can to give your plants a drink or let's spend 10 minutes thinning then we can have a treasure hunt and find some peas to pick."
- It's very important to show off their work. Lots of attention can be the best motivator for children to stay involved in their projects.

- When people come over point out their gardening projects. Take lots of picture to place in their gardening journal and to share with grandparents or other special people in their life.
- Encourage them to talk about their garden and to keep a garden journal. (See the appendix for "Your First Garden Journal)

One of their first gardening projects can be a **simple gardening journal** made with brown paper bags for the cover with separate papers inside, all tied together with a ribbon. This allows you to add more papers or even brown paper bags as needed. In this journal the kids can record what they planted, when the seeds sprouted, which grew first, how they tasted (put a star beside those you would grow again), etc. Your empty seed packs can be placed in the brown paper bag covers for easy reference.

Simple Gardening Journal

Material needed:

1 or 2 brown paper bags

Sheets of paper cut just short of the length and width of the bags so they will easily fit inside the bags.

Ribbon

Hole-punch

Directions:

Fold your brown paper bags in half. If you are using 2 bags, place one bag inside the fold of the other. Punch two holes beside the folded edge. (see image below)

Simple Gardening Journal

Directions (continued:)

Cut your sheets of paper so they are just a bit smaller than the brown paper bags. Fold each sheet of paper in half. Punch holes by the folded edge to match where the holes in the brown paper bags are.

Once you have all your sheets of paper folded with holes punched in them, place them in between the folded brown paper bags and tie a ribbon through the holes to hold your journal together.

Another idea for a **Garden Journal** is to have a binder with photograph sheets placed in it (or buy a photo album.) You can add photos of your garden in there, empty seed packs and use recipe cards to write notes on and add to your journal. With a binder you can just add sheets of paper to write on and even add a calendar that has spaces for you to write in each day what was happening in your garden.

Look for the accompanying Workbook to this book " Bringing Out the Potential of Children. Gardeners" on Amazon or at http://fullpotential.co.place

*Note: Site referenced on October, 2017 at http://fullpotential.co.place

In that workbook I've included special pages for your first gardening journal.

To summarize this beginning chapter –

The focus here was to emphasize to your children that this is their own garden or growing area and to have them involved in all parts of the creation of it. Make sure their growing spot is easily accessible, that there is plenty of sunshine to grow in and it is sheltered from the wind.

Set them up for success by keeping things simple and start small, never rushing and giving them lots of encouragement and attention, stepping in where necessary. Limit the amount of time spent on each task and make it fun!

The next chapter we're going to get down and dirty looking at the foundation of our garden, the soil.

Chapter 2: Soil – Building a Good Foundation

Soil – the foundation of every garden. A good healthy soil makes for good healthy plants.

Let's take a look at what soil you have to work with. Actually take a look.

Have your child dig up a sample of the soil where you want to garden (no soil to work with? Don't worry we'll cover growing in pots and making soil too.) Do a simple soil test as described below. Children are usually fascinated with it.

Take the soil sample that you dug up and put it in a clear jar with a lid (there should be no more than half the jar full with soil.) Fill the jar with water, fasten the lid and let your child shake it up so the soil is well mixed with the water. Set it on the counter overnight and see how the soil settles. Do you see layers as in the picture below?

17

These layers are what your soil is made up of. There can be sand, silt, clay and one other element that shows up, which is humus.

The ideal soil to aim for is loam which is a combination of the three. Ideally you want 20% clay, 40% sand, and 40% silt for plants to thrive in.

Remember this is only what we are aiming for. You can always improve your soil by adding compost, leaves, grass clippings, well-aged manure, plus many others things too!

If you are **growing in pots** pick up a good bag of potting soil or you can mix your own.

Kids love to play in the dirt so now is their chance!

Potting Soil Recipe:

- 2 parts coconut coir or peat moss.
- 1 part finished, sifted compost or sterilized soil. (Sterilize soil by baking the soil at 200 degrees in your oven.)
- 1 part perlite. Some people also use vermiculite or plain old coarse sand in place of perlite in homemade potting soil recipes, too.

Potting Soil Recipe:

Directions:
1. If your coconut coir came in a block, you'll need to hydrate it by putting it in a big container of water.
2. Mix the coir or peat moss and compost or soil. Add more water if you need too. It is much easier to mix if it is damp.
3. Add in the perlite, give it a stir, mixing it all together and you've got your homemade potting soil ready to go!

Compost, gardener's gold, is another great way of improving any soil and for making soil.

There is a magic in taking your food scraps, waste material and turning it into rich, nutrient dense soil to grow more food.

There is a wonderful pdf on composting

* "Composting for Kids"
by Robert "Skip" Richter
County Extension Director – Travis County Texas AgriLife Extension Service. Found at:

http://aggie-horticulture.tamu.edu/kindergarden/kidscompost/CompostingForKids.pdf

Note: * Composting for Kids" referenced on July 13, 2017 at http://aggie-horticulture.tamu.edu/kindergarden/kidscompost/CompostingForKids.pdf

To **make compost** you'll need:

1. Greens (Nitrogen): food scraps, grass clippings, coffee grounds, weeds that have not seeded.

2. Browns (Carbon): Add dried leaves, newspaper, cardboard or sawdust.

3. Water: added to keep the compost moist.

Use a half and half mixture of greens and browns.

The Waste Management Authorities gives out a free booklet * "Do the Rot Thing" all about compost. It has games and an educational component too. It even gets into worm composting (vermicomposting) so kids can start their own worm farm!

Get your free copy at: http://www.cvswmd.org/uploads/6/1/2/6/6126179/do_the_rot_thing_cvswmd1.pdf

Note: * "Do the Rot Thing" referenced July 13 at http://www.cvswmd.org/uploads/6/1/2/6/6126179/do_the_rot_thing_cvswmd1.pdf

Now if you are going to start a **brand new garden plot** try -

   Putting a layer of cardboard down to cover and smother the lawn or any vegetation growing. This will turn it into compost which can be dug into the garden. (Best done in fall and keep on over winter)

   Time for some digging. Get out a garden fork. Let the kids start the process and take turns with them to get it dug down 6" to 12".

   This is the time to build up and enrich your soil. The kids can bring in some compost, shredded leaves or well-rotted manure, which will be good additions to your soil.

21

I want to put a good word in here for collecting leaves which are such a rich addition to your garden. Look at nature, how leaves are shed in the fall to break down and feed the soil for next year's growth. Start your children collecting leaves to feed their garden too!

No Dig Method – Start with your layer of cardboard or thick layer of newspapers and instead of digging down build your garden bed up.

I use what is called the "Lasagna" gardening method (named because of its layers.) Kids love this method! They get to collect and spread different layers in the garden then make little homes on top to put their new plants in.

It's made by putting down alternating layers of compost, old potting mix, well-rotted manure, straw, shredded leaves or grass clippings. Water down each section as you add it. Repeat until you have a garden bed that is about 8 - 12" deep. Finish with a layer of straw or fine mulch on top to keep the weeds down.

When you go to plant your layered garden pull some of the mulch back in a row or dig holes in it to add some compost or potting soil. This is where you will do your first plantings, letting the rest of the garden break down and compost.

Remember to start small. You can always make it a bigger by adding some more layers of material around the edges.

Indoor Garden

Even if you don't have a garden plot, there's no need to miss out on the fun! Rey gardening indoors.

- The same as outdoor gardening you are looking for a place to grow with lots of light. You will need to find a sunny window or supplement your light with grow lights.
- To prep a windowsill garden area make sure you protect the windowsill or table from water damage. You can place your pots in individual saucers or in a large plastic tray to catch drainage.
- Use a good potting mix to grow in.
- Because your plants are growing in containers feed them more and watch your watering (information on fertilizing and watering in following chapters).

In the next chapter we'll be looking at getting those seeds and seedlings into the garden and growing.

Chapter 3: The Miracle of Seeds and the Emerging Seedlings

Where the Miracle Begins!

Here is where the wonderment pops out! Kids enjoy planting seeds, watching them sprout, and eventually producing food they can eat.

Many companies will give out free seed catalogues, which are great fun to look through and find different seeds you may want to grow.

Seeds of Diversity has a whole listing of seed catalogues at:

http://www.seeds.ca/diversity/seed-catalogue-index

Note: Seed of Diversity site was reference on July 15th, 2017 at:
http://www.seeds.ca/diversity/seed-catalogue-index

Hint: Before you get carried away by all the marvelous items to choose from remember you want to keep it small to begin with. Make yourself a list of what you like to eat or what you might buy at a farmers' market. Also consider some edible flowers which make a beautiful addition to the garden.

To help you with your selection I've put down some edible flowers and their uses, some quick and easy to grow snacking plants plus some fun plants to grow that you can actually play in.

Edible Flowers — See which ones appeal to your child. Consider too, what their favorite colors are when deciding which flowers to put in your garden.

- **Nasturtium and marigold petals** with their bright orange colors and spicy flavor are lovely in salads.
- **Borage** adds a nice cucumber flavor to salads.
- **Violets and pansies** are delicious when lightly sugared. Use them to garnish cupcakes or cookies. Also they make for delightful ice cubes along with the borage flower.
- **Sunflower heads** can be steamed and eaten like artichokes while they're still green plus when they go to seed they produce a protein-rich snack.
- **Dandelions** are delicious when battered and fried like fritters. Same applies to the daylily buds.

Easy and quick to grow, perfect for a **snacking garden** some of my favorite **pick-and-eat vegetables**. Remember, if you don't have garden space you can plant these in pots. In just weeks, they'll be ready for picking.

- Radishes (very quick growing. 45 days. Try the Easter Egg variety packs for multi-color radishes)

Easy and quick to grow plants (continued):

- Baby Carrots (you can eat the small ones when you are thinning them out and continue picking them on until freeze up) Make seed tapes (directions later in this section) to get your spacing just right which will reduce the amount of thinning needed. Let the carrot seeds grow to the perfect size for snacking, baby carrots.
- Lettuce (pick your first salad of the baby greens.) Try a variety pack of lettuce seeds for added color and shapes.

More favorite **snacking plants**.

- **Cherry tomatoes** - available in red, yellow, and orange varieties. These are bite sized which makes them great for picking and eating right off the vine. Try a dwarf variety like Patio, Tiny Tim or Window Box Roma. If you can't find the dwarf varieties mentioned here, try anything with the word compact, midget, bush, tiny or teeny in their name.
- **Snap Peas** – a faster growing variety of pea with no need for shelling, you can eat them shell and all.
- **Mini cucumbers** – my favorite snaking cucumber is Cool Breeze. A compact plant that can easily be grown in a container.

Here's another type of **easy and quick to grow plant**:

Herbs (try mint, parsley, or chives) One of the best part of gardening is being able to pick and eat your veggies right off the plants. I've put in these herbs for they can be easily grown in pots on the windowsill and are great for beginner gardeners. Encourage your kids to grab a leaf to eat and add some fresh herbs into your recipes.

- Make mint tea using a handful of leaves. It is wonderful warm or cold.
- Chives are excellent in salads or in scrambled eggs or toppings on soup.
- Parsley is great in soup and I add it in my pesto recipe along with my fresh grown basil.

One more **snacking plant**:

Consider growing some **strawberries**. It's so lovely to pick those sweet berries straight off the vine. Strawberries can be happily grown in pots, but if you have the space for a larger strawberry patch it's better. Strawberry plants spread and multiply substantially from one year to the next. Soon you'll have some extra plants to share with others. H-m-m maybe you have a friend or neighbor with an established strawberry patch that they would be willing to share some of their plants with you to get started.

Fun-favorites for kids to grow and play in.

- **Sunflowers** - These massive flowers grow quickly, and will soon tower over your kids. Plant them around the edges of a square growing area, and voila, a private sunflower house for your children to play in.
- **Pole beans** - Want another hiding spot? Try a bean teepee. Tie three or four 10-foot poles together at the top, forming the basic teepee structure, then plant a few bean seeds around the bottom of each pole. Beans grow really fast, and before long you'll have lots of delicious beans to eat, plus a shady little hide-out.

How about turning your **food scraps into new plants**! Romaine lettuce, celery and green onions easily grow from the parts that you would usually throw away.

Here's how to regrow them:

- **Lettuce** - put the romaine lettuce stumps in half inch of water refilling if needed to keep it at half inch. Do this for a few days until you start to see new leaves starting to regrow, then you can plant them into some soil and grow them in a sunny windowsill.

Growing plants from scraps (continued)

- **Celery** - cut off the base of the celery and placing it in a bowl of warm water in a sunny spot. Watch for new leaves starting to grow in the middle of the base. In about 5 to 7 days the leaf growth will start to thicken and can be planted into a pot of soil and grown on a sunny windowsill.
- **Green Onions** - cut off the base with the roots intact and put it into a container of water in direct sunlight. Change the water every few days and it won't be long before the green part will start to regrow. You can cut off the green part and they will keep growing back.
- **Potatoes** can also be grown from scraps, from the potato peelings. Cut the peelings into two inch pieces with at least two or three eyes on them. Dry them out overnight then plant them about 4" deep in the ground with the eyes facing up. In a few weeks you should see the potato plant starting to grow.

Not quite ready for a garden plot yet?

Here's a quick simple way to get some seeds sprouting for some freshly grown food – **seed sprouts**.

Seed Sprouting

You can sprout beans, peas, lentils, wheat, alfalfa, clover, broccoli, radish, onions and more. The thing about sprouts is that you get to see results happening in days, easily visible in the sprouting jar.

Here's how to do it.

Material needed:
- 1 quart wide mouth canning jar
- some screening or folded cheese cloth cut about the size of the jar opening with an inch overhang. elastic band to hold the screening as a lid.
- 1 canning lid for storage
- 2 - 3 T. of sprouting seeds

Method:
➢ 1. Place seeds in jar, attach your screening. Fill jar with cool water until it more than covers the seeds. Allow to sit over night or about 8 hours.

➢ 2. The next morning, pour out water and rinse seeds really well. Do this several times. Drain well and lay the jar on it's side on the counter.

Seed Sprouting

Method: (continued)

➢3. Repeat step 2 twice a day until sprouted the way you like it. Usually about 3 days but it can be as much as 5. Once the seeds start to sprout move the jar to a spot with indirect sunlight to green them up a bit.

➢4. When the sprouts are nearly done sprouting to the size you want, do not rinse them for a bit so they won't be too damp for storing them to the refrigerator. Store with a cap on.

Take this one step further with growing **microgreens**.

You can grow:

Lettuce
Kale
Endive
Beets
Spinach
Radish
Watercress
Peas

 The best ones to start with are radishes or mixed lettuces for they are fast to germinate and easy to grow.

Micro Greens (continued)

Material needed:

- one or more small plastic food containers, such as those baby spinach or baby greens are sold in
- a small bag of seed starting mix
- one or more packets of seeds
- a drainage plate
- a paper towel

Directions:

Planting Directions:

➢ 1. Poke some small drainage holes in the bottom of the plastic container.
➢ 2. Fill your container almost to the top with seed starting mix soil.
➢ 3. Water the soil until it is very wet.
➢ 4. Sprinkle seeds thickly and evenly across the top of the soil.
➢ 5. Press the seeds gently into the soil.
➢ 6. Drape a damp paper towel across the top.
➢ 7. Place the container on the drainage plate and put it in a sunny window.

Micro Greens (continued)

Care:

Note: may vary with different seed varieties and the conditions they are grown in.

For a few days, once or twice a day, remove the paper towel, mist the seeds, then replace the paper towel.

After seeds have germinated, 3-5 days, remove the paper towel. Continue misting the seeds once or twice daily.

Once the seeds are beginning to take root and leaf out, switch to watering with an increased amount of water just once a day.

After a couple of weeks when the greens have one or two true leaves harvest them by tipping your container almost on it's side and cut the greens off with scissors at the stem. Rinse and enjoy!

Micro Greens (continued)

Want a super simple way to get started growing micro greens –

Try growing some fast growing seeds on a damp sponge. Wet the sponge and sprinkle seeds generously over the surface. Spray gently with water every day. Cut off sprouts for eating when at the desired length.

Have some fun with sprouting seeds by growing **cress heads**.

Material:
- 1 Packet of cress seeds
- Some cleaned half of eggshells
- Cotton balls
- Water

Directions:
Decorate your egg shells putting faces on them
Stuff egg shells with cotton ball 2 or 3.
Sprinkle seeds on top and water.
Place in a sunny window and watch them grow!

Seed Tapes

I mentioned earlier about seed tapes, which cuts down on the thinning and is a fun project to do when you're not able to get into your garden.

Here's how to do it:

Material needed:

- Any type of seeds
- Zip lock Baggies or plastic containers - marked for what type of seed tape will go in it
- 1 Tb Corn Starch
- 1 C Cold Water
- Paper Towels, cut in 1 1/2 - 2 inch Strips and folded in half
- Any squeeze type bottle, (you can wash and use an empty mustard or ketchup bottle)
- A drop of food coloring (optional)

Directions for preparing seed glue:

Dissolve Cornstarch in Water over a medium heat until it boils and thickens. Mixture should look opaque and cling slightly to a fork before dripping off.

Let it cool and transfer into squeeze bottle add 1 drop of food coloring and shake the bottle to make your 'Glue Dots' easier to see.

Seed Tapes

Directions for preparing seed glue: (continued)

Lay out Paper Towel Strips, and place dots across one side of the fold with the cornstarch mixture spacing the dots according to the planting directions of the Seed Packets.

Place seeds on top of the dots, fold other half of paper towel on top and let it dry completely.

Store in a plastic bag or container until you are ready to plant.

Drop the seed packet with instructions in with your seed tapes for future reference.

How to Use Seed Tape

When you are ready to plant your seeds, unroll your seed tape and cut it to whatever length you need for the area you are planting. Place the tape on the soil, and cover it with the amount of soil that the seed packet recommends for planting depth.

Now let's get some seeds in the ground and growing.

Tips for the beginner gardener:
- Check the seed packets for planting instructions.
- Gather all your gardening essentials and have them handy. These may include things like a garden fork, spade. Watering hoses, soaking hose, hoe, hand weeder (remember the old kitchen fork, perfect for this), and a basket for moving around mulch or soil. Make sure you have equipment that the kids can handle.
- Larger seeds are pressed gently into the soil. Smaller seed is usually just 'broadcast' carefully on the surface.
- Most seed should be covered lightly with soil, and the soil should be pressed down gently.
- Water the seedbed thoroughly with a nozzle that makes a gentle spray, then water daily until you see seedlings. A week or so after the seedlings emerge, you can reduce your watering to every other day and water a bit longer each time.

Some things to consider –

- Different plants have different needs for sunlight. Those that need full sun include tomatoes, squash, beans, eggplant, corn, and peppers, while those less dependent on the sun are leafy vegetables, potatoes, carrots, and turnips.
- When choosing what to put where, remember to place taller plants on the north side of your plot to prevent their shadows from blocking the sunlight to shorter plants.
- It's a good idea to mark your rows so you know where everything is growing (or make a little garden map marking where you planted everything. A map is a good addition to your garden journal).

Here's some simple, cheap and cute methods for **making garden markers**

Rock Garden Markers

Material needed:
- smooth medium-sized rocks
- tempera, gouache or acrylic paints
- outdoor varnish

Rock Garden Markers (continued)

Directions:

Have your child paint the rocks with solid colours.

Gouache is non-toxic, washable and has good covering properties. For older kids, which can handle the paint better, acrylic paints are better.

Paint the rocks to match the color of the vegetables example: Orange for carrots, green for lettuce and peas, red for beets.

After the rocks dry add some drawings to symbolize the plants they represent.

Have fun with them like giving them silly faces.

The last step of the project is to varnish the stones, protecting them against moisture. Do it in a well-ventilated area giving the stones two or three coats.

 **Garden Gnome Stick Markers**

Garden Gnome Stick Markers

➢ 1. Using a pocket knife to carve a pointed "hat" (see image) at the top of one end of a twig. Some help may be needed on this part for younger children. Remember to teach safe knife handling before starting.

➢ 2. Carve a rounded, flat "face" on one side of the twig. (see image)

➢ 3. Carve a rounded, flat area on the bottom part of the stick (see image). This is where you will write the names of your plants with perma marker.

➢ 4. Paint your gnomes' hats and beards with craft paint in any color you choose!

➢ 5. Let dry completely then write the veggie names onto the bottom part of the twigs with a permanent marker.

Simplified Twig Plant Marker

Similar to the gnome stick markers just much simpler and no knife involved.

1. Gather up some small branches, about 1/4 to 1/2 inch around.

2. With a vegetable peeler, strip a couple of inches of bark at one end, making a flat surface, and use permanent marker to record the name.

Simplified Twig Plant Marker (continued)

Note: If the wood is green and oozing sap, let it dry overnight before writing.

Even simpler yet use recycled popsicle sticks or plastic fork for markers.

Children find it so hard to wait to see results and to be able to start eating from their garden. Be patient (gardening is great for teaching patients with the wonderful rewards it gives you.)

Here's some expected times for when you can start some of your harvesting.

- Radishes, cress and some lettuce will be ready the quickest in 6-8 weeks.
- Next in line are dwarf beans, cucumber, cabbage, tomatoes and onion which will be ready in 8-12 weeks.
- Most others, including the popular peas, carrots and potatoes will need 16-20 weeks to mature.

The children and you could be harvesting from these little gardens for many months.

Many plants you'll want to grow from seed (the cheapest route to go) or are required to be direct sown (check the seed packs for instructions). To save you time and get a jump on the growing season you can always buy "starts" or seedlings from local nurseries.

* Missouri Botanical Gardens has a site full of growing tips (although it is geared for their specific area it still has many valuable tips that are great for any area.) A good reference site at: http://www.missouribotanicalgarden.org/gardens-gardening/your-garden/help-for-the-home-gardener/edible-gardening/vegetable-gardening.aspx

Note: * Missouri Botanical Gardens website reference July 14, 2017 at the url:

http://www.missouribotanicalgarden.org/gardens-gardening/your-garden/help-for-the-home-gardener/edible-gardening/vegetable-gardening.aspx

Indoor Gardening

- A good place to start is with indoor potted herbs (I had mentioned a few in an earlier section on easy to grow plants)
- Grow in a sunny window or supplement your light with grow lights.
- Have everything handy before you get started. Have pots or containers with adequate drainage and the right depth for the plants you're growing, compost/potting soil, seeds, watering can.
- Decide which plants you want to grow and know their requirements then place plants with similar moisture and sun needs in the same container.

You'll be surprized at what you can grow in containers.

Ideal candidates for container gardens are:

- leaf and head lettuces
- spinach
- green bush beans do well in containers as small as 8" deep and 8" wide per plant. The big seeds of the beans are easy for the kids to handle.
- peppers (may require staking)

Ideal candidates for container gardens (continued)

- onions
- radishes can be grown quickly and easily even if you have the smallest container

Try growing a few of your beans out of the ground so the kids can watch them grow. To do this you'll need your bean seeds, a jar, some paper towels or napkins and water.

Instructions

- Swirl a small amount of water around the jar.
- Fold your napkin or paper towels, dampen them and place in the jar.
- Place the bean seed in the jar resting on the napkin.
- Spray some water on the bean every few days.

The bean should start to grow roots after a few days.

Try growing some **carrots in containers** too, with varieties like: Thumbelina, Short n Sweet or Little Fingers.

Or try growing some **peas in containers**. You can plant up to six plants within a 12-inch deep pot of the following baby pea variety:

Green Arrow

Maestro

English

Grow some fresh and juicy **tomatoes** with the popular dwarf varieties like;

Patio

Tiny Tim

Window Box Roma

A real fun project I started with the kids was to **grow potatoes in a potato grow bag** which had a little flap at the bottom. This flap allowed the kids to reach in and grab some potatoes while their potato plant continued to grow.

Or try a bit of a science experiment starting a potato by sitting your seed potato in daylight until eyes begin to form and leaves begin to sprout. Then, transplant your potato into a 5 gallon bucket or container or better yet, grow them in a laundry basket which will allow you ro see the potatoes as they begin to form and grow. For some added fun try growing some purple potatoes!

A cool system for indoor gardening is an aquaponics system in which an aquarium of pet fish nourishes your plants grown above while the plants in turn clean the water for the fish.

Simple Aquaponics System for your aquarium

Material needed:
- A functioning aquarium
- Plastic storage tub that fits the top of your aquarium
- Grow bed medium – fine rocks or clay beads or anything that can support your plants.
- Standard aquarium pump or any pump for moving the water.
- Overflow valve

Step 1: The Grow Bed

This is where your plants will grow.

Use your storage tube and put in two holes.

One hole for the pump to go through and one as an over flow in case the drain holes fails.

Drill a series of drainage holes along one side of tub opposite to the side where the holes for the water pump and over flow.

Place the tub on top of your aquarium at an angle. The slant will allow the water to flow over

Simple Aquaponics System for your aquarium
Step 1: The Grow Bed (continued)

your growing medium and drain back into the fish tank. Make sure the drainage holes are at the bottom and the two holes for the pump and overflow are near the top.

Wash off your growing medium and place them in the tub (now your grow bed).

Connect your water pump and let the system run to make sure it flows properly and there is no issues.

Step 2: Plants

There are many plants that are suited to aquaponics but green leaf vegetables with low nutrient needs are best. I find lettuce to be one of the best for this system.

The plants clean the water for the fish and the fish in the water give nutrients to the plants.

Step 3: Fish

This will work fine for goldfish or Koi. If you want a fish that you can also have the benefits of fresh fish to eat tilapia is commonly used.

For a more elaborate system designed by Doug McClung of GardenPool.org, a wonderful international public charity for sustainable food research and education there is their shelfponics

The **"Shelfponics"** uses a simple plastic shelf unit placed upside down creating three grow beds which are feed by your 10 gallon aquarium which will fit perfectly on the bottom self.

Find complete instructions for this unit and other interesting DIY projects at *Garden Pool Website. Go to:

https://gardenpool.org/online-classes/introduction-to-shelfponics

Note: * Garden Pool Website referenced July 14, 2017 at: https://gardenpool.org/online-classes/introduction-to-shelfponics

  In the next chapter we will be looking at feeding and watering your plants.

Chapter 4: Feeding and Watering Your Plants

Now that things are planted and growing, it's time to look at caring for your garden. How to give your plants everything they need to flourish and create an abundance of fresh garden produce. M-m-m!

Let your child (now a young gardener) know that plant's just like people need to have food and water. For a lush succulent growth give your plants regular watering.

Watering tips:

- The general rule is to give your plants about 1" of water a week.
- Let that budding young gardener poke their finger into the soil to see if it feel dry. They can stick their finger right in about 3-4" and if it feels dry it's time to water.
- Bring out the watering can or hose. You can also bring out a rain gage for checking to see how much water you are giving your plants plus it's always good to have a rain gage out to measure how much rain your garden is getting anyway. This is a good indicator if you need to water.
- The best time for watering is in the morning.
- Teach your kids not to over water and drown their plants making them waterlogged.

Make your own **homemade water gage**:

What you'll need:
- A plastic (soft drink) bottle
- Some stones or pebbles
- Tape
- Marker (felt pen)
- A ruler

Instructions:
➢ 1. Cut the top off the bottle.
➢ 2. Place some stones in the bottom of the bottle. Turn the top upside down and tape it to the bottle.
➢ 3. Use a ruler and marker pen to make a scale on the bottle.
➢ 4. Pour water into the bottle until it reaches the bottom strip on the scale.
➢ 5. Put your rain gauge outside where it can collect the rain. After a rain check to see how far up the scale the water has risen.

Now you've given them water what about food for your plants. Well feed plants will grow up big and strong just like kids.

Feeding your plants:

- If you have done a good job of improving your soil feeding it with decomposed leaves, compost or maybe you added some well-rotted manure then you will not have to fertilize too much.
- Your plants will tell you if they are lacking something with stunted growth, pale leaves and low yields.
- The best time to feed them is when they are at their most active stages of growth and when they are starting to bloom and fruit.
- If you didn't get time to add compost in when you were preparing your garden you can always make some compost tea to give to your plants. Kids love making concoctions and they can watch their plants come alive and thrive with a good feeding.
- Compost and other plant teas are usually fed to the roots of your plants, simply water into the soil. Foliar feeding can also be done and the helpful microbes and bacteria in the tea aid in combating viruses, fungi, pests and diseases.

- For foliar feeding, grab an old shirt, curtain or piece of muslin to strain the tea before filling up your sprayer or watering can, then add a small squirt (approximately ½ teaspoon of detergent or vegetable oil per watering can - 4 litres/1 gal)) to help the liquid stick to the leaves.

Compost tea from compost

Use a large waterproof 4-5 litre (1 gal) bucket or container with a lid. For ease of making a finer compost tea, put a sack in your container to put the compost in. Fill your container (or sack in your container) half full of compost; including any plant matter that has not fully broken down yet. Top up with water and cover with lid. Leave sit for a few weeks then your compost tea will be ready to use diluted approximately 1:10, or the colour of weak tea. Leave it longer and keep topping it up to use it throughout the growing season or you can start with a fresh batch each time. If you are not using a sack to contain the compost you will have to strain it before using just the liquid.

Here's some added things you can do to improve the quality and potency.

- Use a forked stick or tool and vigorously stir the tea every couple of days.

- To super charge it, spend up to 10 minutes and stir one way to create a vortex then change direction and make the vortex spin the opposite way.
- Aerate it with an aerator you can buy from a garden supply shop or fish and pet supply shop. Follow the instructions to set it up in your container and keep it bubbling away to produce an aerobic tea.
- Add a large spoonful of sulphured molasses as a sugar and micro mineral source.

If you are doing worm composting (instructions were given in the section above on making compost) you can use that to make compost tea or the leachate, the liquid that trickles slowly from the bottom of your worm composter, can be used. Dilute approximately 1 to 10 with water and feed roughly each week on fast growing plants, in the spring and summer, and every 3 weeks for larger slow growing plants.

Now, not only can you make your own compost, you have the know-how for making compost tea for feeding the plants in your garden.

In the next chapter we will be looking at cutting down competition to your plants to make sure it's your special garden plants that are getting all this good food you provided.

Chapter 5: Getting Rid of the Competition - Weeding and Thinning

Like all good mothers who nurture their young, they also protect them too. With our young plants we want them to grow to their full potential. That means getting rid of anything that is competing for your plant's nutrients, sunlight and water.

This is where weeding and thinning comes in. Not always the favorite task for kids. Hint: it helps if they have a hoe of their own just their size for the task. Even add a table fork to your child's toolbox for digging out weed close to their plants.

Some helpful tips:

- Learn to identify weeds and manage them with this handy guide put out by the *National Gardening Association at: http://garden.org/learn/library/weeds/
- catch the weeds when they are young and easier to pull out.
- If it's thinning you're doing, most seed packs will tell you what distance to thin your plant to for best growth.

Note: * National Gardening Association site referenced July 15, 2017 at: http://garden.org/learn/library/weeds/

Chapter 6: Doing Pest Control and Keeping Your Plants Disease Free

A healthy garden is the best defence.

The very best thing you can do for your garden is to check it over regularly, it's a wonderful pest control method too. Make it a regular thing, part of your daily routine. Choose a time that fits into your daily schedule, say after breakfast. Earlier in the day is best, before the heat of the day.

Take a tour around the garden. Check -
- the rain gage to see if the garden got any rain water.
- Look for dry looking plants and check the soil to feel if it is dry.
- Look for any unhealthy plants and watch for any bugs that may be moving in to eat your plants.

Insects and disease are usually attracted to stressed, damaged or otherwise unhealthy plants.

Easiest way to prevent insect damage in your garden is to discourage them from coming in the first place. Instead attract beneficial insects by creating a garden insectary.

* Earth Easy shows you how at: http://eartheasy.com/grow_garden_insectary.htm

To keep your garden healthy -

- Pull out any weak plants.
- Build healthy soil
- Try foliar sprays (mentioned earlier). Seaweed spray is great if you can get it.
- Minimize insect habitat. Clear garden area of debris and weeds which are breeding places for insects. Use clean mulch.
- Interplant and rotate crops. Mixed plantings makes it much less likely for pests to spread throughout a crop. Rotating crops each year helps avoid a re-infestation of pests which might have over-wintered in the garden.
- Keep foliage dry. Do your watering early so foliage will be dry for most of the day. Wet foliage encourages insect and fungal damage to your plants.
- Disinfect. When working with infested plants, clean your tools so you don't spread it.

Note: * Earth Easy website referenced July 15, 2017 at: http://eartheasy.com/grow_garden_insectary.htm

Encourage your kids to take good care of their plants, just like a good mother, watching them closely, catching things early plus giving them everything they need to grow. Do this and they will be well on their way to being a successful gardener and producing healthy delicious food!

In the next chapter we'll be talking about harvesting all that good food they have grown!

Chapter 7: Bringing In the Harvest and Preserving It

At the beginning it was all just a wish and a hope for all that delicious food that would be produced. Now all the fruits of your labor are ready to harvest and bring in to enjoy.

Note: Include the amount of harvesting as part of your garden planning, keeping the garden manageable for your kids. When planning what you will be planting also pick out some favorite recipes your kids would want to use their produce from the garden in or different ways of preserving they might like to try (try small batch canning at first.) Keep in mind how much of their harvest will realistically be eaten.

Make harvesting a routine you can do daily. Have a daily harvest walk. Add to your checklist in chapter 6 - checking for ripe and ready to harvest crops. Give your child a harvesting basket making sure to always keep it handy (perhaps by the door) ready to fill with vegetables. Try to schedule your "harvest walks" before the heat of the day.

Knowing when your crops are ripe and ready to harvest and also knowing the best way to store them has been made easy by the Weekend Gardener Monthly Web Magazine, who published a wonderful harvesting guide to help you with just that.

Apples

Harvest season ranges from midsummer to late fall, depending upon the variety.

Most apples are ready to pick when they separate easily from the tree and the fruit comes off when you give it a gentle lift and twist. Another indicator is the color of the seeds in the core. When apples are ripe, the seeds turn dark brown.

If you're still in doubt, take a sample bite. An underripe apple will taste green or starchy, while ripe apples are sweet and juicy. Overripe apples get mealy.

To avoid pulling out the stem when you harvest, don't yank the apple to pick it; instead hold the apple in your hand, tilt it upward, and twist to separate it from the branch with a rotating motion.

Length of storage varies, ranging from only a few weeks to 6 months depending upon the variety. Store apples at near-freezing temperatures and at high humidity; a good root cellar for storage is ideal.

Asparagus

If you started your asparagus bed from crowns, you should be able to harvest lightly for a week or two in the spring of the second season, but waiting until the third season lets the plants establish healthy root systems.

The third year should bring a moderate harvest for 3 or 4 weeks and then heavy picking for 6 weeks or more every year thereafter.

Pick sparingly the first time - over about 2 weeks. Extend your harvest gradually in subsequent season, until you are harvesting for about 8 weeks. In more temperate climates this can last up to 12 weeks.

Always gauge the length of your harvest by the previous season's growth. Select only those spears that are thicker than a pencil; anything thinner should be allowed to grow into ferns.

Harvest spears in early spring when they are 6 to 8 inches (15-20 cm) tall and the tips are still firm and closed. Cut or snap the spears off at, or just below, ground level. If you opt to cut your asparagus be careful not to injure the plant crown.

When the emerging spears get progressively thinner, it's time to stop harvesting.

Asparagus is best when fresh, but you can refrigerate it for up to 1 week. Set asparagus upright in 1 to 2 inches (2.5-5 cm) of water and refrigerate. Don't let the spear tips get wet, or they'll rot. Surplus asparagus freezes really well, so that is always another option.

For more, use our in-depth Growing Guide:

Growing Asparagus

Beans

You can harvest beans up until frost starts.

Snap Beans
Green, Yellow - come in both bush and pole varieties

Pods should be firm and crisp at harvest and about as thick as a pencil; they should snap when you break one in half. The seeds inside should be very small and underdeveloped, because beans are overmature if the seeds have begun to fill out the pods. Hold the stem with one hand and the pod with the other to avoid pulling off branches that will produce later pickings. You can carefully pinch the pods with your fingers or use a scissors. Pick all pods to keep plants productive.

Shell Beans
Romano, Lima, Southern Peas, Soybeans, Fava, etc. - come in both bush and pole varieties

Shell beans can also be grown as dried beans. Pick these varieties when the pods change color and the beans inside are fully formed but not dried out. Pods should be plump, firm, and tender. Quality declines if you leave them on the plant too long. Pick every couple of days to keep the plants productive.

With both shell and snap beans, you can keep the pods in plastic bags for 1 or 2 weeks in the refrigerator, or freeze the surplus.

Dried Beans
Great Northern, Navy, Pinto, etc.- come in both bush and pole varieties

Let the pods get as dry as possible in the garden, and pick pods of dry beans when they have turned brown and the seeds have hardened. You'll be able to hear the seeds rattling inside the pods. If the weather is too damp for the beans to dry, harvest the plants and hang them upside down indoors.

Pods when thoroughly dry will split readily, making seeds easy to remove. Shell the beans when they are completely dry, and place them in an airtight jar with a desiccant to absorb moisture; store in cool, dry spot for up to a year. Read this article for more about How To Save Seeds

For more, use our in-depth Growing Guides:

Growing Dried Beans
Growing Fresh Beans

Broccoli

Harvest while heads are a deep green, still compact, and before buds start to open into flowers. If the buds start to separate and the yellow petals inside start to show, harvest immediately. Cut the stem at a slant about 4 to 6 inches (10-15 cm) below the head. Removing the head on some varieties will produce sideshoots in the axils of leaves and you can get 4 to 6 cuttings of shoots per plant over several weeks. The thick stems are edible, but they should be peeled first. The leaves are tough, but usable in soups and stews.

When you bring your broccoli inside, soak the heads in a salt water mixture (1 to 2 tablespoons (15-30 ml) of salt per gallon (3.8 l) of water for 20-30 minutes before cooking or storing. This will drive out any cabbageworms hiding in the heads. Broccoli will keep for a week or so in the refrigerator if wrapped in plastic. The best way to store broccoli for longer periods is to blanch and freeze it.

For more, use our in-depth Growing Guide:

Growing Broccoli

Cabbage
Red and Green

Cabbage is ready to harvest when the head is full and firm. Cut the stalk at the base of the head with a sharp knife and discard the outer leaves. It's best to harvest them in the morning, when heads are cool.

After the center head has been removed, small heads may develop where the base leaves meet the stem. Let one of them grow and you'll often get another head weighing around 1 or 2 pounds (.5-.9 kg).

Keep heads in a cold, moist area, just about freezing and around 90% humidity.

For more, use our in-depth Growing Guide:

Growing Cabbage

Carrots

Carrots are generally ready for harvest in 2-3 months or when they are large enough to use.

Pull a few to check their size. Loosen the soil with a fork, and then gently pull them out of the ground. Watering before harvest can make pulling them out easier. Brush off excess soil and twist off the tops.

You can leave carrots in the ground until you need them because even mature carrots will retain their quality in the ground unless the weather gets extremely hot. After the first hard frost, but before the ground freezes, you'll want to harvest the rest of your carrots.

Refrigerate unbruised carrots or layer them in moist sand or sawdust and store them in a root cellar for up to 4 months. You can also can, freeze, or dry carrots.

For more, use our in-depth Growing Guide:

Cauliflower

Pick cauliflower when the heads are full, but before the curds begin to separate. Cut through the stem under the head, leaving a few "wrapper" leaves for protection. Curds bruise easily, so handle them with care.

Before preparing or storing cauliflower, soak it in a salt water mixture (1 to 2 tablespoons (15-30 ml) of salt per gallon (3.8 l) of water for 20-30 minutes before cooking or storing. This will drive out any cabbageworms hiding in the heads.

Cauliflower will keep for about a week in the refrigerator if wrapped in plastic. It does not store well in a root cellar. The best way to store cauliflower for longer periods is to blanch and freeze it.

For more, use our in-depth Growing Guide:

Growing Cauliflower

Corn (sweet)

Look for dark brown, soft silks (not brittle silks), and pick the ears when the kernels are plump and tender and when milky liquid comes out when you prick them with your fingernail. If the liquid is clear and watery, the corn isn't ripe yet; if there is no liquid, the kernels are too ripe and past prime.

Corn tastes best when picked in the later afternoon because of its higher sugar content. Harvest by twisting the ear off the plant in a downward direction. Because the sugar in the corn quickly converts to starch, eat or preserve the corn immediately after harvesting.

The sugar-enhanced or super-sweet varieties hold their sweetness and may be kept in the refrigerator a few days longer than standard cultivars. Freeze or can any surplus corn you may have.

For more, use our in-depth Growing Guide:

Growing Sweet Corn

Cucumber

Cucumbers mature very quickly. Pick them often so the plants continue to produce. Fruits may become oversized if left on the vine even a day too long.

Slicing Cucumbers

Can be harvested whenever they are big enough to use, but before they begin to turn orange or yellow. If your vines bear more than you can use at one time, pick them anyway because allowing them to ripen to the orange stage on the vine will cause the plant to stop producing.

With slicing cucumbers (as opposed to pickling cucumbers) keep fruits picked so that each plant has only 2 or 3 fruits growing at a time.

To pick, hold the stem with one hand and pull the fruit with the other. Harvest fruits when they are young and the seeds inside have not begun to harden.

Cucumbers contain mostly water, so the key to storing them after the harvest is to keep that water in, a reason many cucumbers in supermarkets are waxed. Wrap the fruits in plastic wrap or bag them and they'll keep a week or more in the refrigerator. The best storage temperature is 45 to 50° F (7.2-10° C).

Pickling Cucumbers

Gather pickling cucumbers when they are very young and the seeds are still quite soft, about 4 to 5 inches (10-12 cm) long. If possible, harvest fruits in the morning because they'll be at their firmest condition at this time of day, and refrigerate immediately. Don't wash them until you're ready to use them.

For more, use our in-depth Growing Guide:

Growing Cucumbers

Eggplant

The best eggplant fruits are so young that the seeds are barely visible when you cut them open and are about 4 to 5 inches (10-12 cm) long for standard varieties, a bit smaller for mini types.

The skin should be glossy and tight. If the skin is dull, that is sign the eggplant if overripe and the flesh will be tough and losing its flavor. Overripe eggplant also have black seeds forming inside.

Cut fruits from the plants with 1 inch (2.5 cm) of stem attached, and store them in the refrigerator.

Lettuce

Leaf Lettuce

Leaf lettuce matures about 40 days from seeding. Start harvesting as soon as the leaves are big enough to eat, about 4 to 5 inches (10-12 cm) long. You can pick the large outer leaves or slice the entire plant off about 1 inch (2.5 cm) above the soil line, prompting the plant to send out new growth, which will reach eating size in another 3 to 5 weeks. Harvest in the morning when the leaves are crisp and full of moisture. If your crop begins to bolt or is threatened by a hard frost, harvest the entire plant.

Head Lettuce

Head and romaine lettuce mature about 70 days from seeds and 20-35 days from transplants. When the heads are firm, harvest by cutting the plant to ground level. For crisp lettuce, harvest in the morning and eat that day. You can store most lettuce in the refrigerator for 1 to 2 weeks; iceberg lettuce keeps up to 3 weeks.

For more, use our in-depth Growing Guide:

Growing Lettuce

Melons

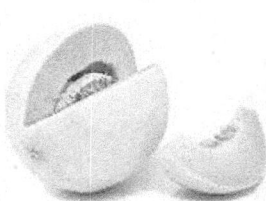

Always allow melons to ripen on the vine.

Muskmelons (also called cantaloupe, rock melon)

Picking muskmelon when they are ripe is crucial to getting good flavor since the plants provide the fruit with much of the natural sugar during the last few days of ripening. Melons that are ripened off the vine (most store-bought melons) just don't taste as sweet.

Muskmelons are ripe when the rind is tan rather than green between the surface netting. Many will have a strong melon fragrance, and the surest sign that the fruit is ready is a crack that forms on the stem right near the point of attachment with the melon. This crack signals the "slip" stage, and in a few days the melon will slip off the vine with minimal pressure. If you have to work to separate the melon from the vine, chances are the fruit is not ripe.

Muskmelons are overripe when the outer skin softens, making it easily penetrable by birds and bees.

Watermelons

When ripe the curled tendril at the stem end dries to brown, the underside of the melon turns yellow or cream-colored, and the melon will give a deep, resonant sound then thumped. The melon's skin also becomes dull and is difficult to penetrate with your fingernail.

Most melons will ripen a little bit more for 2 or 3 days after they're picked. Store melons at room temperature until they are totally ripe, then refrigerate for several weeks. Melons can be pureed or cut into pieces and frozen.

Honeydews

The number 1 mistake home gardeners make is picking honeydews too early. Keep a record of your variety's maturity date and keep the melons on the vines at least until then, a bit longer if you've had a cool spell during the season. They will improve for a few days after picking if kept at room temperature.

For more, use our in-depth Growing Guide:

Grow The Juciest Melons Ever

Bulb Onions and Garlic

Bulb Onions

You can begin to harvest onions as soon as they are big enough to use as green onions.

Bulbing onions are fully mature when the tops turn yellow and start to fall over. To speed the maturation process, knock the tops over with back of your rake, just bending them over, not snapping them. Wait a few days until the tops turn brown, then carefully lift the bulbs out of the ground with a spading fork. Gently brush off the soil, but don't wash them.

To reduce the risk of rotting in storage, cure the bulbs by letting them dry in a warm, airy place out of direct sun or rain for a week or two. When the papery outer skins are completely dry and brittle and the tops are withered looking, cut the tops off about 1 inch (2.5 cm) about the bulb and put them in mesh bags or braid the tops together. Hang braids or mesh bags of onions in a cool, dry spot to store them.

Garlic

Harvest when leaves begin to turn brown. Pull several bulbs and break them apart. If it's too early, cloves will be unsegmented and difficult to separate. Leave the remaining bulbs for a week a two, and check again. If you leave bulbs in the ground too long, the outer skins begin to deteriorate, resulting in lower quality and poor storage. A rule of thumb is to harvest when 75% of the foliage is brown.

Use a pitchfork to harvest the bulbs, and let them dry outside in the sun for a few days, then store in a cool, dry place. You can braid the dried leaves and hang the bunches or trim away the leaves and roots, and put into mesh bags and hang them in a well ventilated room.

Pea Snow and Snap

Peas are ready to pick about 3 weeks after flowers appear. Harvest plump pods that are just beginning to look bumpy; if the pods are discolored or shriveled, the peas are past their prime.

The best time to harvest is early in the morning because the pods are crispest then and will store better and stay fresh longer.

Use scissors to cut pods from the plant, or pull them off very carefully or you may uproot the plant. Try and harvest daily to keep the plants productive.

It is always best to eat fresh peas immediately because, like corn, their sugars turn to starches very quickly. Refrigerate extra peas for up to one week in brown paper bags that are then put inside a plastic bag and seal with a twist tie. The paper bag will absorb any extra moisture so that the peas aren't actually sitting in water, and the plastic bag holds in enough moisture so the peas stay fresh. You can also freeze or can them.

For more, use our in-depth Growing Guide:

Pear

Pears should be harvested when they are mature, but still hard, and ripened **off** the tree for best eating and canning qualities. If you wait until the fruit is ripe on the tree, it will be mushy inside within a day or two.

A pear is ready for harvest when the green color lightens and the stem of the fruit parts easily from the spur when you lift up on the fruit with a slight twist.

Allow pears to soften and ripen indoors at a temperature of 65-70° F (18-21° C).

Check the neck for ripeness. To do this, apply gentle pressure to the stem end of the pear with your thumb. When it yields to the pressure, it's ready to eat (this process usually takes a few days depending upon the variety, some may take a few weeks).

For storage, keep fruit at a high humidity and near freezing. The length of storage varies with each different cultivar.

Pepper

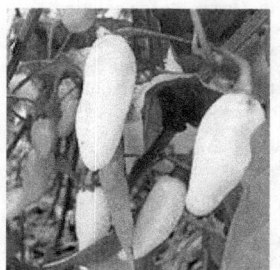

Begin harvesting when peppers reach a usable size. Steady harvesting after that will keep plants producing new fruits.

Most peppers can be eaten when they are green and underripe, although the flavor and vitamin C content improves as they ripen on the plant.

Cut bell peppers from the plants with a sharp knife or pruning shears, leaving at least ½ inch (1.3 cm) of stem attached. Cayennes, and some other peppers usually come off with enough stem attached when pulled from the plants. Always use a scissors or shears if you find yourself having to twist and tug to get peppers picked. You don't want to break or damage the delicate branches.

Ripening will continue after harvest if kept in a warm room; ripening stops when peppers are refrigerated. Most peppers change color when ripe. Small, thin-walled peppers, like cayennes, tend to color up quickly. Sweet bell peppers can show strips of yellow, red, or orange and will continue to ripen when harvested and stored at room temperature.

Store thick-walled peppers in plastic bags in the refrigerator for up to 2 weeks, or wash, cut into strips, and blanch them for 30 seconds in boiling water, and freeze them. You can also pickle peppers if you want.

Small-thin-walled peppers start drying the moment you pick them. To dry hot peppers like cayennes, lay them in a single layer in a very warm place until they are beyond leathery but not quite crisp. Then store them in airtight jars.

Potato

As tubers become fully mature, the potato plant's stems and leaves turn brown. You don't however, have to wait for the plants to die back to start eating your potatoes. Harvest when the potatoes reach the size you want. If you plan to store them, make sure the skins are very tough, and don't peel off easily when you gently rub them with a finger at harvest time.

If your soil is loose, simply pull up the brown foliage and use your fingers to explore the soil and find more potatoes. You can also use a pitchfork to gently loosen the soil and lift the tubers out by hand.

Leave the potatoes outdoors for an hour or two to dry off on the ground. There's no need to wash or brush them before storing, although you can wipe away any clumps of soil. Keep the potatoes in complete darkness after they've dried in the open for a short time. Don't leave them in any container that light can penetrate or the potatoes will turn green.

If you plan to store your potatoes, you'll be better off if you cure them for a week or two. Put potatoes in a single layer on newspapers in the dark around 50-60° F (10-15° C) for 2 weeks to cure. After curing, store in boxes or bags at about 40° F (4.4° C).

Pumpkin, Winter Squash
Summer Squash, Zucchini

Pumpkins and Winter Squash

Harvest pumpkins and winter squash when the rind is hard enough to resist puncturing with a fingernail, or wait until the plants begin to die back. When handling any kind of pumpkin, try not to pick it up by the stem because if the stem gets broken off, this is a weak spot for decay.

Cure winter squash and pumpkins in a warm (75-80° F (24-27° C), dry, well-ventilated place for 10 to 12 days.

After curing, you may want to dip them in a weak bleach solution (10 parts water to 1 part bleach) to kill fungi and bacteria on the skin and prolong storage. Allow to drip dry and then move pumpkins and winter squash to a cool, dark, dry, and well-ventilated storage area where temperatures range between 50-55° F (10-13° C). Don't store in a damp root cellar.

Spread squash out singly or, if you have to stack them, try not to do more than 2 deep so they have plenty of air circulation and don't rot.

Summer Squash and Zucchini

Harvest summer squash when immature and still tender, and not more than 6 to 8 inches (15-20 cm) long and 2 inches (5 cm) in diameter. Harvest patty pan, or scallop types when they are 3 or 4 inches (7.6-10 cm) in diameter. Keep plants harvested to prolong production of fruit.

Harvest all squash by cutting fruits with 1 inch (2.5 cm) of stem attached. Pick summer squash when they are small, harvesting every day because fruit quality deteriorates with age. Store in the refrigerator.

For more, use our in-depth Growing Guides:

Tomato	
	Tomatoes are ripe when they change color. For best flavor, harvest tomatoes when firm and fully colored. Some cultivars drop their fruits when they are ripe, just pick these up and use them. Store at room temperature, never store tomatoes in the refrigerator because cool temperatures cause them to lose flavor and textures. For more, use our in-depth Growing Guides: Growing Tomatoes Growing Tomatoes & Tomato Growing Tips How To Ripen Green Tomatoes

Thank you to Hilary Rinaldi, a certified organic grower, and a member of the National Garden Writers Association. She is a nationally published writer, and regularly speaks and writes about all gardening related topics concentrating on making gardening fun and successful for everyone.

Sourced July25, 2017 Weekend Gardeners Monthly Web Magazine

http://www.weekendgardener.net/vegetable-gardening-tips/harvest-090709.htm

This work is licensed under a Creative Commons Attribution-NoDerivs 2.5 License.

https://creativecommons.org/licenses/by-nd/2.5/

Five Ways To Preserve and Store Produce

Preserving and storing food is becoming a bit of a lost art and it's a shame. What do you do when you have a bumper crop of green beans, squash or tomatoes? There's only so much of any one food you can eat before you get sick and tired of it. If you know how to preserve it, you can put it up and use it throughout the year.

Freeze It

A great place to start is by freezing food. You can cook up your harvest in some of your favorite freezer friendly foods, or clean and precook them and toss them in the freezer. This is also a great way to store fruits like berries and peaches that don't last long once they are ripe. The only disadvantage to freezing food is that you're limited by the amount of room you have in your freezer. Be sure to get in the habit of labelling frozen food well so you know what it is before you pull it out to thaw and how long it's been sitting in the freezer.

Five Ways To Preserve and Store Produce (cont.)

Can It

Canning is one of the most versatile ways to preserve food. You can make and can anything from jelly and pie filling to chili and green beans. Canning has the added advantage of not taking up any space in your fridge and freezer. You can store your canned goods in the pantry, on a shelf in the kitchen, or anywhere in the basement. Heck, I've been known to keep canned goods stuck under the spare bed if I'm running out of room. Properly canned food also stores a lot longer than any other method.

Dehydrate It

If you don't have a lot of space, consider dehydrating food. You can start by using your oven on the lowest setting. Try dehydrating some apple slices, or any type of food to use in baking and cereal throughout the year. Then explore further and come up with fun snacks like kale chips, banana chips and even dried veggies that you can use in soup.

Five Ways To Preserve and Store Produce (cont.)

Herbs can be quickly dried in a dehydrator but for an even simpler method consider air drying them.

- If you want to air dry your herbs, keep about 5 or so branches together in a bundle, securing them with a rubber band. Keep in mind that smaller bundles are going to dry a little faster. Now take your herbs and put them in a paper bag, with the stem side up. Close the bag and tie it off, poking some holes in the bag carefully. Now hang it in a room with lots of rooms for proper ventilation. This shouldn't take longer than a week.

If you don't have a dehydrator try oven drying the herbs

- If you want to get your dried herbs into containers by tomorrow, using the oven is the ideal method to try out. Start by turning on your oven and setting it to 180 degrees Fahrenheit. Let it pre-heat while you prepare your herbs to be dried. Once it is preheated, you can put the herbs on a pan and then bake it at 180 for up to 4 hours, but at least 2 hours. This does remove a little bit of their flavor, so keep that in mind when you decide to bake them.

Five Ways To Preserve and Store Produce (cont.)

Pickle It

Another favorite old-fashioned way to preserve food is to pickle it. Pickling involves submerging the produce in a brine made of salt, sugar, water, and various pickling spices. The most common pickled item is of course pickles and it's a great place to start. But don't stop there. You can pickle peppers, okra, cauliflower and a wide variety of other veggies and even fruits. Play with it and see what you like. Pickled veggies make a great addition to sandwiches and salads throughout the year.

Cold Store It

Last but not least let's talk about the simplest way to store food. Things like root vegetables, apples, and cabbages store well in a dry, cool, and dark place. This used to be the reason any house had a root cellar. Today your pantry might be a good place to store this type of food. If you're lucky enough to have a basement, you can set up some shelves to keep a lot of produce for months to come.

Easy Ways To Get Started With Canning

Canning at first glance sounds like one of the scariest ways to preserve food. With freezing, you toss food in freezer bags and store it in your deep freezer. With dehydrating, you stick it in a machine that slowly dries it out. With canning though, you need a canner, canning jars and there's always the possibility that jars explode. Honestly though, canning isn't as scary as it sounds. Buy quality glass jars, follow directions to a "T" and you'll be just fine.

A fun place to start is by making jelly or jam. Pick your favorite fruit, find a jam or jelly recipe and give it a try. You need some half pint glass jars and tongues that will allow you to grab hot jars out of boiling water. Dig around and see if you have a pot large enough to hold the jars and get started. Follow the recipes and directions and you'll do fine. Any jars that don't seal properly should go in the fridge and be used right away.

Another great place to start is to with a simple vegetable canning project. Canning green beans is very simple and you can use the beans throughout the year in any dishes you'd use store-bought canned beans. Clean, cut, and blanch your green beans to get them ready for canning. Then follow canning instructions to make sure you cook them long enough and get

Easy Ways To Get Started With Canning (cont.)

them to a high enough temperature to kill any bacteria and create a good seal. As with any type of canned good you should store jars that didn't completely seal in the fridge and use them within the next couple of day.

Another great option is pickles. If you have a bunch of cucumbers growing in the garden, or want to try your hand at some sort of other pickled vegetable (like cauliflower, peppers, or okra for example), give canned pickles a try. The vinegar solution already does a great job preserving the food. Canning ads even more time and allows you to store vegetable that would otherwise go back quickly even longer.

Stay away from canning meats or high acid produce like tomatoes in the beginning of your canning career. Those can be a little trickier to can successfully. Get a few batches of canning under your belt, and invest in some good canning gear (including thermometers and proper canning pots before giving these types of canned goods a try.

Simple Tips For Freezing Fresh Produce

One of the easiest things to do when you have more fresh produce than you know what to do with is to freeze it. A surprisingly large variety of fruits and veggies can be frozen "as is" or you can wash and chop them into a form that's easy to pull out and cook with down the road. This won't take long and will make cooking that much easier when it's time to use these yummy foods. Cutting fruits and vegetables also allows you to pack them in tighter, giving you more space in the freezer.

Let's run through a couple of things you may choose to freeze. Berries are one of the easiest fruits to freeze and they are best frozen whole. Keep them in the freezer, then pour them out as needed to top oatmeal, make smoothies, or bake a pie. Other fruits like peaches, bananas, and pineapple for example freeze really well, but it's much easier to peel, and chop them first. Apples and pears don't freeze well unless you turn them into pie filling first. Grapes can be frozen, but don't thaw well. If you have too many grapes, toss them in the freezer and eat them frozen.

Simple Tips For Freezing Fresh Produce (cont.)

Lots of veggies can also be rinsed, chopped and frozen. Green beans, peas, squash, broccoli, cauliflower and the likes freeze very well. If you see it in the frozen food section at the grocery store, chances are it will freeze well. Just rinse the produce as it comes out of the garden or from the farmers market, chop it and put it in freezer bags. You can even freeze potatoes if you peel and grate them first. Peppers and onions do well chopped and frozen. Don't forget to label everything really well.

Tomatoes can be a bit tricky. If you don't have the time to do anything with them right away, chop and freeze them and then use them to make salsa or to make pasta sauce and tomato soup down the road. You can also just pop whole frozen tomatoes in a freezer bag and prepare them as you use them. If you have a bit of extra time on your hands, I find you get much better results cooking the sauce or soup now and then freezing it. This also makes it much easier to put together a meal down the road.

Fresh herbs can also be frozen. Some herbs like dill, parsley or chives can just be popped into a freezer bag and a portion chopped off when you need it.

Simple Tips For Freezing Fresh Produce (cont.)

Another easy way to do it is to wash and chop your herbs and scoop them into ice cube trays. Top them with water, chicken broth, or olive oil and freeze until solid. At that point you can pop them out of the ice cube tray and put them in a freezer bag for longer storage. Rinse and repeat as needed. Throughout the year whenever you want to brighten the flavor of a dish, just add one of the frozen herb cubes to the pot.

A Quick Guide To Getting Started Dehydrating Food

Dehydrating or drying out food is one of the oldest food preservations out there and something that's making a bit of a comeback in recent years. The idea is to preserve the food by removing as much of the moisture or water content as possible. Not only will this keep fruits, vegetables, and even meats from spoiling, it also removes a lot of the weight and size of each piece of food. This allows you to store your harvest more easily. Many dehydrated foods can be eaten as is, but you can also soak them in water or another liquid to rehydrate them.

A Quick Guide To Getting Started Dehydrating Food (cont.)

The reason dehydrating works so well to preserve a large variety of food is because yeast and bacteria need water to grow. By removing all the water from the food, there's no way for these microorganisms to thrive, thus leaving your food well preserved. You can dry food in the hot sun, in the oven, or with a dehydrator. The oven is a great place to get started, while a dehydrator will give you better control and lower settings that result in tastier dried foods.

The optimum temperature for drying food is 140F. This can be a little hard to hold even on the lowest setting on your oven. Before you start to do any dehydrating in the oven, I recommend you invest in an oven thermometer. It will help you determine what the actual temperature in your oven is. It will also allow you to turn the heat on and off as needed to stay at or close to the ideal dehydrating temperature. The same thermometer can also be very helpful when you're starting to experiment with solar drying. Of course you won't need it if you invest in an electric dehydrator.

Play around and start drying some fruits and vegetables. Get comfortable with the process and more importantly, see how you and your family enjoy the dry food.

Different Ways To Make Jellies and Jams

One of the most popular ways to preserve fruit is as jellies or jams. Those fruit spreads can then be used throughout the year on toast or bagels. Of course jellies and jams also make a great addition to your oatmeal or muffin and you can even cook and bake with them.

The Difference Between Jelly and Jam

The basic process for making jellies and jams involves combining the ripe fruit and sugar to turn it into a fruit spread or preserve that won't spoil. The sugar and heat work together to preserve things. There is a difference between jelly and jam.

A jelly is a spread made from just the juice of the fruit, while both flesh and juice are used to make jam. The process is very much the same. To make jelly, you simply add one step that involves straining out the juice before proceeding to through the rest of the process. This process involves cooking the fresh fruit with sugar and, if needed, a little acid like lemon juice. Once everything is cooked down (and the juice is strained if needed), a jellying agent like gelatin is added, the hot mixture is add to jars and allowed to cool.

Freezer Jams Are A Great Place To Start

A fun place to start your jam making adventure is with freezer jam. Most recipes call for nothing more difficult than fresh fruit and sugar. You cook them to make a jam that's then frozen until you're ready to use it. It's a quick and easy way to put up fresh berries. Keep one container of jam in the fridge to use right away and store the rest in the freezer. These types of jam are quick and easy to make. Perfect when you don't have a bunch of fruit to put up and you have the freezer space to store the extra containers. While you can use glass jars, there's always a risk of the glass busting when it is frozen. It's safer and easier to use plastic jars when making freezer jam.

Canning Jellies and Jams

Your next step on the jelly making journey is to prepare traditional jellies and jams that are canned for long term storage. Since there is only so much jelly you can consume in a given week or even month, it makes sense to choose a preservation method that allows you to keep the fruits of your labor for a year or longer. That's where canning comes into play. You will make a batch of jelly or jam, ladle the hot fruit mix into canning jars and then process them in a hot water batch. Follow your canner's direction for processing the finished canned jellies and jams.

How To Decide What To Can, What To Freeze And What To Dehydrate

When it comes to preserving fresh produce, you have options. You can freeze it, dehydrate it, or can it. What preservation method you choose will depend on a variety of different factors.

Start by figuring out what your options are. Green beans for example freeze and can well, but don't particularly lend themselves to dehydrating. Bananas on the other freeze and dehydrate well, but you don't really can them. Apples dehydrate well, but have to be processed into apple sauce or pie filling before you can or freeze them. Berries are delicious frozen, dehydrated, or turned into jam and frozen. Spend a little time doing your research if you're not familiar with the preservation methods that lend themselves to a particular fruit or vegetable.

Once you know what you can do with a particular food, think about how you like to use it later. If you love to add dried fruits to your oatmeal or granola in the morning, it makes sense to dehydrate those berries. If you prefer them in smoothies, freeze them instead. The same goes for any other vegetable. If you love pickled cauliflower as a quick veggie side or on a sandwich, it makes sense to pickle and can this yummy vegetable. If you prefer it steamed or

How To Decide What To Can, What To Freeze And What To Dehydrate (cont.)

use it to make soup or mock mashed potatoes, freezing it makes more sense.

Your last consideration should be space. Each of these preservation methods has different requirements. The first place you'll likely run out of room is the freezer. If you think this may become an issue, keep that in mind as you try to decide if you should freezer or dehydrate or can something. For example if you have a bumper green bean crop, and find it quickest and easiest to freeze them, you may want to consider canning a batch or two at the top of harvest time to make sure you have room left in the freezer for some other things. If you don't plan ahead, you may end up with a freezer full of green beans.

With canning your main restriction will be the amount of jars you have. Thankfully canning jars are fairly inexpensive and you can add a pack each year as needed. Of course you also need a cool, dark place to store the finished jars full of canned goods. When you run out of room in the pantry, get creative. If you have a basement, you should have plenty of extra room. If you don't consider storing the jars in a closet, or even under the bed. While those may not be ideal locations, they greatly expand the amount of

How To Decide What To Can, What To Freeze And What To Dehydrate (cont.)

room you have to store canning jars.

Dried or dehydrated food will take up the least amount of room. It's also by far the lightest. This makes it a great option when you're starting to run out of room. Just remember that you need a plan for consuming all this dehydrated food down the road. You can store the dry food in airtight bags, plastic containers, or glass jars.

How And Where To Store Your Produce To Make It Last

Yes, you can preserve your produce by freezing it, canning it, cooking it, pickling it, or even dehydrating it. But sometimes, you just want to keep it around to use up for a few days, weeks, or even months. Let's talk about what you should store where to make sure it lasts and stays fresh as long as possible.

People used to have a root cellar. One of the reasons it got that name is because root vegetables store well in a cool and dark space. If you have a cool pantry, or even better a dark, dry basement, you can store things like potatoes, sweet potatoes, carrots, onion and the likes there. Apples also store very well in a place like that as do cabbages

How And Where To Store Your Produce To Make It Last (cont.)

Mostly leafy vegetables do best in the fridge. Bring them home, wash them, dry completely. Wrap them in a paper towel and store them in a plastic bag in the fridge. If you don't have a dry, dark place for your cabbage and apples, they can also be stored in the fridge.

What you store next to each other also makes a big difference, especially in a close space. Remember the old trick of sticking an apple or banana in a brown paper bag with some unripe fruit? The same thing happens if you keep all your fruit in a bowl on the counter, or in a bag. Most fruit and things like tomatoes do better out of their container, spread up on the kitchen counter.

Another important tip is to never store your onions and potatoes together. While they both benefit from dry, cool, and dark spaces with plenty of air flow, the onions give off a gas that makes potatoes sprout and rot much faster than if they are stored away from onions.

While most produce will stay fresh and tasty the longest when stored in the fridge, there are some foods that should not be refrigerated.

How And Where To Store Your Produce To Make It Last (cont.)

They include:
- Tomatoes
- Avocados
- Bananas
- Kiwi
- Pineapple
- Peaches
- Apricots
- Mangos
- Nectarines

These fruits (yes, tomatoes and avocados are technically fruits) tend to become mealy when they are stored at too low of a temperature. Keep them on the counter instead.

By paying attention to what produce likes to be stored where, you can not only extend how long it will keep without any major efforts to preserve the food, it also preserves the flavor. And that's really the point, isn't it? To keep food fresh, flavorful, and packed with nutrients until you're ready to cook with it and eat it.

The Benefits Of Pickling Fruits and Vegetables

Pickling is one of the oldest forms of food preservation. It involves submerging the food in either vinegar or a salt brine to keep it from spoiling. Spoiling is a process that involves bacteria, and not all bacteria are created equal when it comes to spoiling or preserving food.

The goal with pickling is to prevent the bad bacteria from growing. In the case of using vinegar to pickle, the high acidity of the vinegar prevents most bacteria from thriving, thus preserving the food as long as it is submerged in the vinegar solution.

With brine pickling, controlled fermentation is encourage like in the case of sauerkraut and kimchi. This allows beneficial bacteria to grow, who then crowd out any bad bacteria that will cause the food to spoil. The interesting thing is that the look, texture, and flavor of the food changes. The same thing happens with cheese by the way, which is fermented milk. Fermented foods make a great addition to your diet. The beneficial bacteria in these foods are healthy for you and help you improve the bacteria that live in your gut. This in turn has a beneficial impact on anything from your digestion to your immune system.

The Benefits Of Pickling Fruits and Vegetables

In other words, eating pickled foods on a regular basis is good for you and your overall health. Pickling is also one of the more cost effective ways to preserve food. And the same type of food can be pickled in a few different ways. Let's take pickled cucumbers for examples, one of the most popular pickled foods in the US (at least if you consider the variety of different pickles in the grocery store).

Kosher pickles are the perfect example of cucumbers being preserved in a vinegar solution. Most dill pickles on the other hand are preserved in a brine. While that mixture may include vinegar, it also includes dill and other pickling spices and salt.

Sauerkraut is another great example of fermented food, as is Kimchi. Fermented pickled vegetables can be found across the globe and it's a preservation method that has been used for thousands of years. There's no need for power, cold temperatures, or special equipment. As long as you have salt, you can figure out a way to ferment and preserve your harvest in one form or another. It's a fun and interesting aspect of food preservation to get into. Since each culture fermented different types of foods and in different ways, there are all sorts of different dishes to explore.

Eating Local and Seasonal Year Round With Old Fashioned Food Preservation Methods.

Summer and early fall are a great time for getting into eating local, seasonal food. But what do you do when the gardens and farms around you stop producing as much food? Depending on where you live, you may still be able to get fresh produce late into fall and even early winter. Milk, eggs, and fresh meat may be available year round. But what do you do about fruits and vegetables during the coldest winter months and early spring before gardens start to produce?

You prepare for it by preserving the summer and fall harvest to use throughout the winter months. Start simple. If you go blueberry picking or are finding a great deal at the local farmers market, freeze some to use in your smoothies and oatmeal throughout the year. Take the family apple picking this fall and pick apples that store well, or make apple sauce. If you have extra green beans or okra, freeze them.

If you're feeling a little more ambitious, consider doing some canning. Most vegetables can well and you can even make a batch or two of homemade tomato sauce and can. Think about what veggies and foods you use throughout the year that you buy canned. These are the first things you want to can. The same principle

Eating Local and Seasonal Year Round With Old Fashioned Food Preservation Methods. (cont.)

works for freezing. What frozen fruits and vegetables to you end up using when you don't have good fresh options at the grocery store? These are the things you want to start with.

From there you can start to explore and experiment. Try making a batch of fruit jam, or try your hand at pickling cucumbers. Talk to farmers and other shoppers at your local farmers market and farms. Do a little research online, or pick up a food preservation book at your local library. And let's not forget about older friends and family members. Grandma cooked mainly from local, seasonal food back in the day and can give you quite a few tips to help you get back to this way of cooking and preserving food.

Don't overwhelm yourself the first year. Do what you can and try a couple of new things. From there, start expanding each year. Try growing more of your food in your garden or pick up a few bushels of corn and put them up the following year. Keep adding a few more things each year and it won't take you long to eat mainly local seasonal food throughout the year.

Chapter 8: Reviewing Your Successes and Planning for Next Season

Once the harvest is in, the garden has been cleaned up and put to bed, it's time to pull out your gardening journal (you did keep one right?) Sit down with your child and review your successes in the garden.

- look at things you would change, what was successful, what needed more improving.
- take note of things you really liked in the garden and want to grow again.
- also what were the things you didn't like and will not be planting again.

Soon the new seed catalogs will be coming in and it will be time to start planning your next year's garden.

Pull out a sheet of paper and draw your garden on it plotting out what you would plant next time in your garden plot.

Find a Free Vegetable Garden Planner with kid vegetable garden at:

http://www.vegetable-gardening-online.com/child-vegetable-garden.html

Note: Vegetable Garden Planner was referenced August, 2017 at: http://www.vegetable-gardening-online.com/child-vegetable-garden.html

ABOUT THE AUTHOR

Patrice Porter

A Mother, Grandmother.

Certified Educational Associate with 10 years experience working with young children in the "Play and Exploration" program.

Gardening Consultant, sharing in her love of gardening and near 40 years gardening experience.

Patrice enjoys her peaceful life in the boreal forest but also enjoys the freedom and connectedness that has come about through her online ventures.

Patrice, truly believing in the potential of our youth and is happy to present her new series of books:
"Bringing Out The Potential In Children"

Look for them at: http://fullpotential.co.place

Appendix 1: "From the Ground Up"

I've included a copy of my booklet "From the Ground Up" for some more information for beginner gardeners (although not specific to children) Enjoy!

Preface

This book will get you started growing nutritious wholesome food in your garden and creating abundance around you.

SITE AND SOIL

First, choose a garden spot that gets at least 6 hrs of sunlight and preferably some protection from the wind. Then you want a good healthy, nutritious rich soil, which is your foundation of all the growth which will take place in your garden. Healthy soil produces healthy plants, less susceptible to pests and disease. In your soil you want a good mixture of rich humus material and dense coarser material for the ultimate mix. A sandy loam is ideal. It holds onto water and plant food but it also drains well, and air moves freely between soil particles down to the roots. Adding compost or well-rotted manure will benefit any type of soil. Also check the pH of your soil. If the pH level is below 6, the soil is too acidic, and you need to add ground limestone. If the measurement is above 7.5, the soil is too alkaline for most vegetables, and you need to add soil sulfur.

SEEDS AND SEEDING

Onto the seeds, check the seeds for their germination rate. There is nothing worse than putting in all the effort of planting and caring for the new planted seeds and have nothing come up. This can be done by putting 10 seeds in between damp paper towels placed in a plastic bag. Keep this in a warm spot and check regularly to see if they have sprouted. Preferably 8 of the 10 seeds germinated giving you an 80% germination rate. Small seeds like onions, carrots, lettuce, and parsnips will only keep for a couple years at best so buy fresh seeds of these. Some seeds will keep for 5,10,20 yrs. To keep seed for many years, they must be protected from heat and moisture. A cool dry area around 50 degrees will keep larger seeds for many years. Cooler temperatures will extend seed life, as long as the seeds are protected from all moisture. You can collect your own seeds from open pollinated plants for future years' planting. Again, save the best seeds from the best plants. When setting up your garden plan to place taller crops on the north and west sides of the garden so they will not shade shorter plants. Check seed packs for the recommended distance between the plants and plant accordingly. Make sure to check seed packages too for the right depth to plant your seeds.

SEEDS AND SEEDING

The rule of the thumb is about three times the width of the seed. Once planted, they need water, you can wait for the rains to come but once they receive some moisture, it's important not to let them dry out, especially tiny seeds like lettuce and carrots, which are close to the surface. Carrots take a long time to germinate, so make sure to keep them moist.

WATER AND FERTILIZER

Once seeds have sprouted above the soil, it's time for regular watering. A general rule of thumb is to give them at least one inch of water a week. Your finger is a good indicator of when the soil has dried sufficiently to re water: Dig down several inches into the soil; if the soil is dry to your touch 3 to 4 inches down, it's time to water. It's best to water in the morning when possible for disease problems are more likely to get started overnight on cool, wet leaf surfaces. You want to make sure you're doing deep watering - water deep into the soil, so the new seedlings will develop deep roots. Vegetable plants and fruits are 75% to 95% water. Succulence, eating quality, plant growth, and productivity are all improved with sufficient moisture levels but do not over watered. If the soil is waterlogged, roots die from lack of air.

WATER AND FERTILIZER (cont.)

You may consider fertilizing too. Plants will tell you if nutrients are lacking by stunted growth, pale leaves, and low yields. The best time to feed plants is when they're at their most active in terms of growing. Typically, this is when you're preparing beds, transplanting seedlings, and when the plants are setting out blooms and fruiting. Plants like corn, spinach, broccoli and cabbage, especially those whose leaves are eaten, are heavy feeders. Legumes like beans and lentils, and medium-leafed vegetables like okra need moderate amounts of fertilizer. Herbs feed sparingly. Fertilize according to package.

WEEDING AND THINNING

As your seedlings start to grow, it's important to keep the competition down, so that your desired plants will grow to their full potential. It's much simpler to weed when the weeds are small and can be easily removed with a hoe. If you have trouble weeding around small seedlings, use a table fork to gently pull out awkward little weeds. It's important too, to thin your seedlings after they develop two sets of true leaves, thin out those that stand too close thin your seedlings after they develop two sets of true leaves, thin out those that stand too close together. Gently pull extra seedlings without disturbing the ones you want to keep.

WEEDING AND THINNING

Some things like carrots you may want to thin later so your thinnings will be big enough to have as your first harvest. Check seed packs for the recommended distance between plants and thin accordingly.

MULCHING- Once you've done your weeding, it's a good idea to apply a mulch (newspaper, straws, old leaves or landscape fabric are great mulches.) Lay down organic mulch when the soil starts to warm and when the plants need regular water. If you mulch too early, the soil stays too cold and wet for proper root growth. In areas with short growing seasons, you can plant broccoli, cauliflower, and cool-season plants through black plastic. Clear plastic warms up the soil quickly, but it also helps weed seeds to germinate, so don't use it. Cover the plastic with organic matter when the weather warms to keep the soil cool for those cool season plants. Black plastic is good for weed control and warming soils. It can be used on many vegetables including cucumbers and squash. Landscape fabric is another inorganic mulch. It doesn't warm the soil as much as black plastic, but it's permeable, enabling you to water through it. It also does a good job of keeping down weeds. Mulch keeps the weeds down and the moisture in, keeping the work load down.

DISEASE AND PEST CONTROL

Start with prevention! Insects and diseases are attracted to stressed, damaged or otherwise unhealthy plants, so the key to preventive control is taking good care of your plants. That means paying close attention to them and providing the conditions they need for healthy, vigorous growth. Choose disease-resistant varieties. Don't overcrowd your plants. Watch moisture levels. Practice crop rotation. Be sanitary. Clean your tools. Inspect your plants regularly and often. Check for bugs, disease, moister levels and catching things early before any real damage is done. As gardeners, we can learn to tolerate some damage to our plants, but use this damage as a signal that the plants might need more attention. It's much easier to pull off a few affected leaves, than to have your whole crop infected.

HARVESTING AND PRESERVING

Once the plants start producing, it's important to keep them picked, that for a lot of plants keeps them producing. Close to the end of the season, you may want to let some of the plants start to produce seeds for your future crops. Also, picking them at the opportune moment when fully ripe gives you the best produce for your labor.

HARVESTING AND PRESERVING

There is nothing like a fully vine ripened tomato or a melon ripened on the vine. Once you start harvesting then it's time to start putting up your harvest, for it all can't be eaten right away.

Herbs can be hanged to dry or dried in bags. Some herbs like dill and parsley are best bagged and frozen to maintain their flavor. A lot of vegetables can be blanched and frozen; berries can be frozen as is. Same as tomatoes or they can be canned. Lots of veggies are great pickled. Try more than just cucumbers as dill pickles. Dilled beans, carrots, asparagus, they are all great tasting. Dehydrating is another way of preserving your garden harvest. It's a great method for maintaining the nutrients value. Also it uses very little space to keep your produce. Root veggies can be dug and stored in a cold room, or an old fridge. Many root crops can be stored in the ground on into winter if you cover them with a thick organic mulch like straw. Applied before the ground freezes, the mulch keeps the soil loose and unfrozen so you can dig the vegetables later into winter. Some root crops are better if they undergo a light frost which sweetens them, and parsnips can be left in the ground for the whole winter and harvested in the spring.

EXTENDING THE HARVEST

Extending your growing season to get the most out of your garden may be done by successive planting. For those crops which reach maturity quickly plant multiple crops every 2 weeks throughout the growing season extending the harvest. Also using row covers to protect from temperatures below freezing or having covers handy to cover plants when there is a risk of frost extends the season. Growing in a greenhouse will definitely extend the season, or even a covered garden will give it enough protection to carry through some cold weather.

CLEAN UP AND PREPARING THE SOIL

Once the crops are finished, clean up the old plants and put them in the compost. You can now prepare the ground ready to get an early start on next season's gardening. When preparing your soil: dig deep. Most plants are content with 6 to 8 inches of good ground for their roots to grow in. If you're planning to grow substantial root crops (carrots, parsnips, turnips, beets, etc.), go deeper still — up to a foot or more. Then fill 'er up. Add lots and lots of organic matter! Try using compost, shredded leaves, well-rotted manure, or a mixture. If your yard happens to be blessed with fertile soil,

CLEAN UP AND PREPARING THE SOIL (cont.)

adding organic matter is less crucial, but most soils can stand the improvement. Do it at this time so it has time to break down releasing nutrients for next year's crop. You can even plant some cold season seeds (lettuce, radish, spinach, etc.) right away for a real early crop.

REVIEWING YOUR SUCCESSES AND PLANNING FOR NEXT SEASON

Once your harvest is all in, and the garden is cleaned up and prepared for the next season it's time to put your feet up and review your successes of the year or things that you want to change. Soon the seed catalogues will be coming in and it will be time to start planning the next year's garden.

May your gardens produce an abundance of wholesome, nutritious food, with an abundance allowing you to share your bounty. Happy growing!

Appendix 2: Garden Recipes

I've selected some simple recipes for you to try with your garden harvest.

Recipes included are:
Brined Vegetables
Strawberry Freezer Jam
Spinach Dilly Dip
Strawberry, Spinach, Cantaloupe Salad
Spanakopita – Spinach Phyllo Pie
Parmesan Baked Swiss Chard Stems
Easy Cheesy Spinach Pie
Oven Baked kale Chips
Roast Potatoes with Dill and Green Onions
Easy Leek and Potato Soup
Roasted Beet Salad with Feta
Roasted Kabocha Squash
Eggplant Fries – Baked Not Fried
Oven-Roasted Radishes

Brined Vegetables

Ingredients

- 1 pound of your favorite root vegetables
- 1 medium red onion
- 2 cloves garlic
- 1 cup of your favorite fresh herbs
- 2 teaspoons black peppercorns

Items Needed

- 2 Tablespoons Pickling salt
- 2 quarts purified water
- 1/2 gallon jar
- 8 oz jar
- Clean cloth and rubber band

Directions:

With a large bowl at the ready scrub and peel the root vegetables. Slice into very thin rounds. Add to the bowl.

Thinly slice the red onions and garlic. Add to the bowl with root vegetables and then add the black peppercorns and whole herbs to bowl tossing everything together.

In another bowl, add the pickling salt into 2 quarts water. Place vegetables in a clean 1/2 gallon jar. Pour the salt water over the

Brined Vegetables

Directions (cont.)

vegetables until covered by 1 inch.

Take the empty 8oz jar and place it on top of the vegetables to act as a weight. Put the clean cloth over mouth of 1/2 gallon jar. And then put the larger jar on a plate and store in a cool (65-75 degrees) place.

Take a look at the jars each day to make sure the liquid stays at least 1 inch over the vegetables.

You'll see the fermentation start in about 24 hours. You should see little bubbles in the brine. There may also be a white film which is a natural, safe yeast that can be wiped out of the jar.

Leave the vegetables for 3 -7 days to ferment. You can check to see if they're ready by tasting a slice of vegetable. Once the vegetables taste the way you like then remove the 8 oz jar, wipe jar rim and cover with a lid. You can store these fermented, pickled vegetables in the refrigerator up to 1 month. Makes about 1.5 quarts

Strawberry Freezer Jam

Ingredients:
- 4 cups strawberries, cut in half
- 4 cups sugar
- ¾ cup water
- 1 package (1 3/4 ounces) powdered fruit pectin

Directions:

Mash up the strawberries until slightly chunky to make 2 cups crushed strawberries. Mix strawberries and sugar in large bowl. Let stand at room temperature 10 minutes, stirring occasionally.

Now, mix the water and pectin in 1-quart saucepan. Heat to boiling, stirring constantly. Boil and stir 1 minute. Pour hot pectin mixture over strawberry mixture; stir constantly 3 minutes.

Immediately spoon mixture into freezer containers, leaving 1/2-inch headspace. Wipe rims of containers; seal. Let stand at room temperature about 24 hours or until set.

You can store the freezer jam in the freezer up to 6 months or in refrigerator up to 3 weeks. Thaw frozen jam and stir before serving.

Dilly Spinach Dip

Ingredients:

- 1 10 oz. Pack of frozen chopped spinach (thawed and squeezed dry)
- 1 cup low fat cottage cheese
- 1 cup low fat sour cream
- 2 tsp. Dried dill
- ½ tsp. garlic powder
- ½ tsp. onion powder
- Cut up vegetables for dipping (ex. Carrots, celery, broccoli, summer squash, etc.)

Directions:

Squeeze water out of thawed spinach. Place in bowl.

Puree cottage cheese and sour cream in a blender or mash with a fork until most of the lumps are removed.

Thoroughly mix spinach with the moist mixture, using a fork to break up the spinach pieces.

Add seasoning and mix thoroughly.

Let sit in the fridge for 2 hours for flavours to blend.

Serve as a dip with cut up vegetables.

Variation: for seasoning use an Italian dressing mix, onion soup mix or vegetable soup mix.

Spinach – Strawberry – Cantaloupe Salad

Ingredients:
- 4 cups fresh spinach
- 1 cup bite sized pieces of strawberries
- 1 cup bite sized pieces of cantaloupe
- Poppy seed dressing or a raspberry vinaigrette

Directions:

Wash and prepare spinach, strawberries and cantaloupe.

Toss spinach and fruit pieces together in a large bowl.

Dress lightly with dressing of choice.

Serve immediately. Refrigerate any leftovers.

Spanakopita – Spinach Phyllo Pie

This Greek dish is filled with spinach and is perfect served with tzatziki. You can serve it as an appetizer or a main dish.

This recipe makes 5 individual serving pies.

Ingredients:

Olive oil

1/2 bunch spinach

4 chopped green onions

1 egg

1 tablespoon Fresh or 1 teaspoon dried dill

1/2 cup crumbled feta

5-10 sheets phyllo dough

How to Make It:

Preheat your oven to 350 F. Prepare your baking sheet by brushing it with olive oil and set aside.

Remove the stems and clean your spinach thoroughly before starting. Squeeze the leaves to remove the liquids from the plant and squeeze them until they appear wilted.

Chop the spinach and put in a large mixing bowl with the green onions, egg, dill and feta.

Spanakopita – Spinach Phyllo Pie

How to Make It (cont.)

Mix until well combined. Get 1 or 2 phyllo sheets and lay them flat on your clean counter. Rub a little olive oil on each sheet and place 1/5 of your filling near the bottom of the sheets.

Fold in the sides of the sheets and then roll them up. Place on your baking sheet with the seam of your roll up facing down. Brush the top with a little bit of olive oil. Repeat 4 more times.

Bake for 20-25 minutes or until golden brown. Serve with tzatziki dip.

Parmesan Baked Swiss Chard Stems

If you've ever booked Swiss chard and wondered what could be done with those fabulous looking stems, look no further. Here's a recipe adapted from Kalyn's Kitchen. Note* Site referenced August,2017 at:

https://kalynskitchen.com/baked-swiss-chard-stems-recipe-with/

Ingredients:

Swiss chard stems, cut in 1 ½ inch pieces

Pepper

Parmesan cheese

How to Make It:

Preheat your oven to 400 F.

The stems are quite hard, so they need to be softened before baking them with the parmesan. Place them in a pot with boiling water and boil for about 5-6 minutes.

Drain the water and place the stems on a non-stick or greased baking surface. Then sprinkle with pepper and Parmesan or other hard cheese and bake in a 400 F oven for about 15 minutes or until the cheese is melted and starting to brown.

Serve warm and eat as an appetizer or as an accompaniment with your meal.

Easy, Cheesy Spinach Pie

Preparation Time: 15 minutes

Cooking Time: 35-45 minutes

- 1 10-oz package frozen chopped, spinach (thawed, and squeezed dry)
- 4 oz reduced-fat cheddar cheese, shredded (1 cup shredded cheese)
- 3 Tbsp fresh onions, very finely chopped, or to taste
- 1 tsp minced garlic (fresh or from jar), or to taste
- 1 cup reduced fat biscuit mix
- 2 cups low-fat or fat-free milk
- 4 large eggs, beaten
- Nonstick cooking spray

1. Preheat oven to 375 degrees Fahrenheit, with oven rack in lower position.
2. Spray the bottom of 9-inch pie pan with nonstick spray.
3. Remove as much water as possible from thawed spinach. Wash hands thoroughly and squeeze handfuls of thawed spinach over sink or bowl. Place squeezed spinach into pie pan.
4. In pie pan, break apart clumps of squeezed spinach. Mix shredded cheese, onion, and spinach together with fork until evenly mixed.
5. In medium bowl, gradually combine biscuit mix with low-fat or fat-free milk. Using whisk, mix ½ cup of low-fat or fat-free milk at a time into biscuit mix, so mixture blends evenly. 6. Thoroughly mix beaten eggs into biscuit mixture.
7. Pour biscuit mixture evenly over spinach mixture in pan.
8. Place pie pan in oven on lower rack and bake 35-45 minutes until golden brown and a knife inserted in middle of pie comes out clean.

Remove pie from oven. Let pie set 5 minutes. Cut into slices and serve.

Variation: Use muffin tins to make individual pies. Spray 24 muffin tins with nonstick spray. Spoon a tablespoon of the spinach cheese mixture in each muffin tin, dividing the mixture evenly among the tins. Pour 1½ tablespoons of biscuit mixture over the top of each muffin tin, dividing mixture evenly between tins. Bake for 15-20 minutes. Make mini pies by spooning a heaping teaspoon of the spinach-cheese mixture into a nonstick-sprayed mini muffin tin. Pour 1/2 tablespoon of biscuit mixture over top. Bake for 10-12 minutes. Recipe makes 24 muffin-size or 48 mini-size muffin pies.

Oven-Baked Kale Chips

They may not be potato chips, but they're a close second. These crispy and nutrition-packed chips are sure to be gobbled up quickly.

Ingredients:

One bunch kale cut in bite sized pieces
Olive oil
Salt and pepper

How to Make It:

Preheat your oven to 325 F. Wash the kale thoroughly and rip it up into bite sized pieces, discarding the stems.

In a large bowl, toss them in olive oil, salt and pepper. You can get creative with the seasonings, if you'd like.

Spread the leaves on a large baking sheet, being careful not to overlap the pieces. Bake for about 20 minutes or until they're crispy.

Roast Potatoes with Dill and Green Onions

A great roasted potato is the perfect complement to just about any meal. These ones include dill and green onions and are very easy to make. This makes about 4 nice sized side dishes.

Ingredients:

8 medium yellow potatoes, cut in half

2 chopped green onions

2 tablespoons olive oil

2 tablespoons fresh chopped dill

Salt and pepper

How to Make It:

Preheat your oven to 350 F.

In a large mixing bowl, add the green onions, olive oil and dill. Add the potatoes and toss to coat thoroughly. Sprinkle with salt and pepper to taste.

Bake for about 50-60 minutes and toss every 15 minutes or so, so they brown evenly on all sides.

Variations:

Use this method to make any kind of flavor combination you'd like. Vary the type of potatoes, herbs and more. Below, is a picture of red potatoes with onions, marjoram, salt and pepper.

Easy Leek and Potato Soup

Ingredients:

2 tablespoons olive oil

2 carrots, peeled and chopped

2 stalks celery, chopped

2 medium onions, peeled and chopped

2 cloves garlic, grated or minced

2-3 leeks, cut lengthwise, then rinsed and sliced

4-5 medium potatoes, peeled and diced

7-8 cups of vegetable stock

A handful of spinach or other greens, chopped

Salt and pepper

How to Make It:

Heat the olive oil in a large pot over medium high heat. Add the carrots, celery, onions and garlic and stir to coat with oil. Jamie Oliver recommend putting the lid on askew and letting the ingredients cook for about 10 minutes this way. Add the potatoes and soup stock and bring to a boil. Reduce heat to medium, put on the lid on the pot and cook for another 10 minutes.

Finally, add the spinach or greens and let cook for another 3 minutes or so, until they have softened. Season with salt and pepper and serve.

Roasted Beet Salad with Feta

Next time you roast beets for dinner, roast a few extras, so you can enjoy this salad the next day. You can used canned whole beets for this recipe too, but fresh is always best. If you need to roast your beets, cover them in foil and put them in a 400 F oven for about one hour. Chop the ends of the beets and peel them while they're still warm.

This recipe makes 4 salads.

Ingredients:

4 medium roasted beets, diced

2 tablespoons hemp, olive or other salad oil

2 tablespoon lemon juice

1 tablespoon fresh chopped lemon thyme

Optional: Field greens or lettuce mix

1/4 cup crumbled feta

1/4 cup pine nuts or chopped walnuts, pecans, etc.

Salt and pepper

Roasted Beet Salad with Feta (cont.)

Instructions:

Combine the beets, oil, lemon juice and lemon thyme in a mixing bowl. If you don't have lemon thyme, you can use fresh basil, oregano or regular thyme. Dry herbs will also work, but use them sparingly.

Get 4 serving bowls ready and add a bed of mixed greens, if you're using them. Top with the beet mixture. Sprinkle with feta, pine nuts, salt and pepper.

Roasted Kabocha Squash

Kabocha squash has a nice dense texture. You may substitute other squashes with similar texture in this recipe which is for delicious squash wedges with honey balsamic glaze. Just use your fork to remove the flesh from the skin as you eat and enjoy.

Ingredients:

1 kabocha squash (or other dense textured squash)

2 tablespoons olive oil

3 tablespoon honey

2 tablespoon balsamic vinegar

Instructions:

Preheat your oven to 400 F.

Wash the outside of the squash, since you will be serving the squash in its shell. Cut into wedges.

Mix the olive oil, honey and balsamic vinegar in a large bowl. Toss in the wedges to coat.

Place the wedges on a greased or non-stick baking sheet, with the flesh facing up. Brush the extra dressing over the wedges. Bake for 30 minutes or until soft.

Eggplant Fries – Baked, Not Fried

If you've tried fried zucchini sticks and fell in love, you're in for a real treat. The best news is, these eggplant fries aren't actually fried. They're baked! They crispy and include a great herb mixture that is sure to satisfy. Serve with marinara sauce or a spicy mayo.

Ingredients:

1 medium eggplant

2 eggs

1 1/4 cups breadcrumbs

1 cup grated Parmesan

1 teaspoon oregano

1 teaspoon basil

Coarse salt and pepper

Eggplant Fries – Baked, Not Fried (cont.)

How to Make It:

Put your rack near the top of your oven and make sure there is space for your baking sheet and eggplant. Set the oven to the broil setting.

Cut your eggplant into wedges, making them fairly thin, so the eggplant will soften when you broil it. Set aside.

Whisk the eggs into a shallow bowl or baking dish. Set aside.

Combine the breadcrumbs, Parmesan, oregano, basil, salt and pepper in a shallow bowl or baking dish. Set aside.

Oven-Roasted Radishes

For many people, the only way they've tried a radish is raw and often, just chopped in a salad. But did you know that radishes taste great cooked? They're marvelous and this roasted radish recipe proves it.

Ingredients:

Radishes
Olive Oil
Fresh Oregano
Salt and Pepper

How to Make It:

Preheat your oven to 375 F.

Remove the greens from your radishes and clean them thoroughly. You can save the greens and sauté them, if you'd like. Then slice the radishes in half and place them in a mixing bowl.

Oven-Roasted Radishes

How to Make It (cont.)

Finely chop the oregano and it to your mixing bowl. Use as much oregano as you'd like, depending on the amount of radishes you have on hand. You can also substitute dry oregano or other herbs, if you prefer. Experiment with the flavors for best results.

Coat the radishes and oregano lightly in olive oil and place on a baking dish.

Add salt and pepper to taste.

Place in your oven for about 20-25 minutes, or until radishes are softened and start to brown. If you have larger radishes, you may want to increase your cooking time.

BRINGING OUT THE POTENTIAL IN CHILDREN SERIES

- Volume 1 - Bringing Out the Potential In Children Writers/Authors
- Bringing Out the Potential In Children Writers/Authors Workbook
- Volume 2 - Bringing Out the Potential In Children Gardeners
- Bringing Out the Potential In Children Gardeners Workbook
- Volume 3 - Bringing Out the Potential In Children Cooks/Chefs
- Bringing Out the Potential In Children Cooks/Chefs Workbook

Find them at the Full Potential Store – http://fullpotential.co.place

Also find this complete series along with the **Companion Workbooks** for each of the volumes in the series **"Bringing Out The Potential In Children"** on Amazon and other fine book stores.

Other Books by Patrice Porter

The Coffee Break Author

Get past that barrier of having no time. Now we make time with "The Coffee Break Author" which breaks down the writing process into coffee break size sessions taking you step by step to the completion of your book.

Available at: http://bringoutthepotential.com

Afraid? Not Me! How I Came to Love My School and the People In It.

A children's book created by Patrice and her granddaughter, Ffion.

It's Patty's first day at school and she's a bit scared. Luckily she has Cuddles, the bunny, and her sister Ava to make her first day a wonderful day. Follow Patty's first day of school in "Afraid? Not Me! How I Came to Love My School and the People In It."

Found on Amazon and other fine book stores

Patrice Porter
Certified Educational Associate
Website:
http://fullpotential.co.place

www.ingramcontent.com/pod-product-compliance
Lightning Source LLC
LaVergne TN
LVHW020934090426
835512LV00020B/3353